CONTENTS

Ships in Focus Publications

Correspondence and editorial:
Roy Fenton
18 Durrington Avenue
London SW20 8NT
020 8879 3527
rfenton@rfenton.demon.co.uk

Orders and photographic:
John & Marion Clarkson
18 Franklands, Longton
Preston PR4 5PD
01772 612855
shipsinfocus@btinternet.com

Printed by Amadeus Press Ltd.,
Cleckheaton, Yorkshire.
Designed by Hugh Smallwood, John
Clarkson and Roy Fenton.

SHIPS IN FOCUS RECORD
ISBN 978-1-901703-94-8

SUBSCRIPTION RATES FOR RECORD

Readers can start their subscription with
any issue, and are welcome to backdate it to
receive previous issues.

	3 issues	4 issues
UK	£24	£31
Europe (airmail)	£26	£34
Rest of the world (surface mail)	£26	£34
Rest of the world (airmail)	£31	£41

SHIPS IN FOCU
March

CW00664103

We apologise that 'Record' 47 appeared about █████ publication date of November 2010. One of th██████ elective surgery, and this inevitably disrupted t.. .... may also delay forthcoming books. We thank both readers and contributors for their patience and for the good wishes they have sent.

This seems an appropriate point to outline what is involved in putting together an issue of 'Record', and indeed our other publications.

In our early days we commissioned articles, but now almost all come unsolicited, largely from authors who have agreed the content and extent of the piece with us beforehand. Although we exercise quality control, especially with first-time contributors, we rely on the authors to get their facts correct. We may be able to add extra data, especially to fleet lists, but encourage authors to make as complete a job as possible. Captions are often our own work, although these and all editorial changes are agreed with the author. The author's presentation of the text, both physically and grammatically, is a vital factor in deciding whether it is accepted for publication. A digital file, or at the very least a clean copy which can be scanned, are usually essential. To minimise sub-editing, we also encourage adherence to our style sheet, copies of which are available on request.

Although the editors themselves contribute features, these are on subjects that appeal to us. From time to time readers make suggestions for subjects they would like to see covered. However, unless we know a potential author able to undertake the work, we tend to encourage those making the suggestion to tackle it themselves, offering advice and assistance where appropriate.

Our major input is to the photographic content of 'Record', where we endeavour to provide the best, comprehensive coverage from our own sources and those of other collectors, whose contribution is vital and greatly appreciated. The scanning of photographs and laying out of the articles is done in house. This is an economic necessity, but also gives us very tight control of design.

The above processes also apply, but on a larger scale, to our other books. Needless to say, taken together with proof checking by authors, editors and third parties, the work is very time consuming. With our commitment to three issues of 'Record' each year, this limits the number of books we can produce, especially as much of our distribution is also done in house.

None of the above should be taken as discouragement to potential authors of articles for 'Record', or indeed of possible books. However, we are particularly selective about taking on new book titles, and at least half the submissions to us are turned down because they are outside the zone in which we feel comfortable. In addition, authors need to be aware that their projects have to take their place in a queue, and that unforeseen circumstances can delay publication.

John Clarkson   Roy Fenton

March 2011

On 5th April 1978 Elder Dempster's *Dunkwa* was photographed in Birkenhead Docks wearing the funnel colours of charterer Cameroun Shipping Lines of Douala. *Dunkwa* and her sisters feature on pages 202 to 205. *[Paul Boot/J. and M. Clarkson collection]*

The almost yacht-like *Aureol* of 1951 was Elder Dempster's last mail boat, seen here in 1955. Sold in 1974 and renamed *Marianna VI*, she worked as an accommodation ship at various locations until laid up at Perama. She was broken up at Alang in June 2001. *[J. and M. Clarkson]*

Onitsha's 150-tonne derrick has lifted on board a very substantial river craft in this photograph from October 1969. Note how the load required the derricks at the second mast to be stowed against the superstructure. Trucks and other vehicles are carried on the after deck. *[Ships in Focus]*

Fleet in Focus

ELDER DEMPSTER POST WAR   Part 2
Andrew Bell

Elder Dempster long had experience in shaping the cargo ships of their fleet to the demands of the West African trade. Almost first among their design priorities was the ability to load southbound general cargo at two ports for discharge at as many as ten ports. The shape of their ships meant that they had a warehousing aspect: it was no use having all the cargo from Liverpool for Lagos in one hatch. Lying alongside Apapa Quay the ideal was to be discharging from all five hatches at any one time to lessen the time in that port, or at any other. The general cargo in those five hatches might well be varied in volume and in value: dried Icelandic fish was not stowed next to bales of printed textiles woven in Manchester; coinage, currency, essential oils and mail had to be in secure stowage in a strong room and every item discharged accounted for by tallying. Northbound no commodities were carried in bulk: tropical produce was never homogeneous other than vegetable oils, some types of which required heating in transit. Sawn timber and whole logs claimed an increasing share of northbound space; the logs being stowed, well lashed down, on deck, or in lower holds leaving 'tween decks for bagged cocoa, sawn timber or crates of valuable timber veneers. All these varied demands were met within the shape of the hull with the cargo spaces having robustly scantlinged lower holds: always one 'tween deck and, in the older designs, an orlop or lower 'tween deck.

Southbound items of capital equipment, which ranged from railway locomotives to electrical transformers and generators, were stowed under deck where possible. Other than the unlikely event of loading in one port for discharge in only one port, all cargo stowage planning was a challenge on which the successful conclusion was always arrived at through collective experience. The highest form of this art was 'half hatching' where cargo for one port interfaced, sharing space with that of others. When the financial results of the voyage had been calculated in the form of revenue earned per day from which running costs per day were subtracted, they could be swung from surplus to loss by thoughtless cargo stowage resulting in slow handling or even claims for cargo damage.

The 'O' class
Responding to the expansion of trade between Britain, Northern Europe and West Africa, Elder Dempster had a continuous newbuilding programme in the 1950s and into the 1960s. From the company's resident Naval Architect and the shore-based engineering management, both having offices on the Sixth Floor of India Buildings in Liverpool, came a succession of 14 cargo ships in three groups from the same drawing boards that produced the elegant passenger ship *Aureol* (14,083/1951) and the sister cargo ships *Eboe* and *Ebani* (9,396/1952). This sequence commenced with the five 'O' class all built by Harland and Wolff at Belfast

where those with a long memory would have recalled that 20 years earlier amidst the Kylsant crash (1930-1931) Sir Frederick Reebeck had been left with the *Achimota* (9,576/1931) the mailboat flagship for which Elder Dempster were unable to pay. This time it was different: five ships ordered, built and paid for in cash.

The first of the 'O' class was the *Onitsha*, taking her name from the strategic entrepot market city on the banks of the River Niger of which someone colourfully but accurately wrote 'only the moonlight sleeps'. Delivered in June 1952 the *Onitsha* was equipped with a 150-tonne heavy lift derrick serving number 2 hatch. Elder Dempster had always had a heavy lift ship in its fleet and it was planned that the *Onitsha* would replace the *Mary Kingsley* (4,017/1931) (see Ships in Focus 'Record' 19). For the whole of her operational life the *Onitsha* was used, in addition to her role in the operational general cargo carrying fleet, to carry special heavy lift items commencing with steam locomotives and ending with that essential structure of industrial offshore oil production, the single buoy mooring. Probably the most unusual consignment of all was carrying, on deck, another Elder Dempster vessel. This happened in 1954 when the riverine ferry *Itu* (129 grt), built by Yarrows on the Clyde, was cut in half amidships after delivery and was carried by the *Onitsha* in two pieces to Lagos where the company's local yard rejoined her on the Government's slipway. The tiny ferry then made the coastal voyage to Calabar, sailing for the next fifteen years on the local oil rivers. The end of passenger carrying in 1966 virtually coincided with changes to the cadet training syllabus at which time the accommodation of *Onitsha* was modified and used by first and second trip cadets.

The second of the class, delivered in November 1952, was the *Obuasi* in which Elder Dempster followed the example set by Blue Funnel and their *Calchas* (7,436/1947) by manning the ship with 18 deck cadets in place of the usual complement of seamen. There was a linking coincidence between the two training ships which was seen in the *Obuasi* being named on 24th June 1952 by Margaret Glasier, the wife of Malcolm Bruce Glasier CBE who had served Blue Funnel as their Marine Superintendent in London until 1951, when he was recruited by John H. Joyce to join Elder Dempster's board as the company's Ships' Husband. Having served his time as an apprentice in sail and then joined Blue Funnel's sea staff, it is generally thought that it was Malcolm Glasier's influence with Lawrence Holt (the senior partner in Alfred Holt and Co.) that made the *Calchas* concept happen. This development was the climax of Lawrence Holt's interest in cadet training, which he had started in 1916 with some revolutionary ideas which rapidly resulted in a quality of personnel that became the benchmark for officer training in the British Merchant Navy.

Mary Kingsley, in charge of two Preston tugs, arriving at Preston on the 18th September 1954 for breaking up. *[D.B.Cochrane/ World Ship Society Ltd.]*

In appearance the first three 'O' class had a family resemblance to the two 'E's but they had short, higher superstructures which had a tidy, rounded, even appearance and which - being higher - was topped with a squat funnel. Carrying 12 passengers on their own deck, that Elder Dempster feature that might be associated with the days of colonial living - the large, airy verandah at the after end of the passenger accommodation - made its last appearance as a design feature on the first three 'O's.

The *Owerri* of 1954 was the last Elder Dempster cargo ship built to carry 12 passengers, for the concluding pair, *Oti* and *Ondo*, both delivered in 1956, appeared with one deck less of the midships superstructure where the passengers' lounge and 16 ensuite cabins would have been. The *Oti* deserves a place in the history of making merchant shipping safer for she was the first ship to have installed the Pyrene-ED Hoi inert gas generating system to smother a fire in a cargo space with a combination of nitrogen and carbon dioxide. This was an idea that John H. Joyce and Technical Director Alan Bennett had developed in partnership with Pyrene, the world-renowned British maker of a range of fire fighting appliances. The nightmare that haunted Elder Dempster as carriers of large amounts of combustible tropical oil seeds was a deep-seated fire that could not be extinguished because the ship had exhausted all the carbon dioxide bottles onboard. It worked: before the ship left on her maiden voyage from Liverpool numerous displays featured a 44-gallon drum with contents ablaze which was lowered into an open hatchway to be totally extinguished in 15 minutes by a blanket of concentrated exhaust gas piped from a pocket-sized plant located in the centre castle. So simple was this concept in its design and working that no attempt was made to patent or copyright the invention. The greatest contribution that it has made is to ensure the safety of empty oil tankers.

If an innovative feature of the *Oti* was a triumph, the loss of the *Ondo* on 6th December 1961 was a tragedy. Approaching the western entrance of the Kiel Canal where the Elbe flows into the North Sea and laden with a cargo of Nigerian cocoa destined for Soviet Russia, the *Ondo* was driven ashore whilst trying to create a lee for the capsized Cuxhaven pilot boat. Despite this selfless attempt the pilot and nine men were drowned. Attempts to refloat the *Ondo* were abandoned in March 1962. Although Captain W.L. Farquhar was dismissed his unsuccessful attempt to save ten men had him feted by the local communities.

As Ocean's influence in the affairs of Elder Dempster grew there was a change in strategy to concentrate on serving only the larger main ports and services to the smaller ones were abandoned. Calabar followed Tiko off the sailing schedules. No longer was the world's finest cocoa loaded at Fernando Po. Shebro had to truck its piassava to Freetown. No longer did the smaller ships fit into the fleet, and in just two months in mid-1972 all four of the 'O' class were sold, and in came competition that saw the opportunity of busting the company's historic and effective monopoly.

Daru and the 'D's

So profitable were the Henderson 'K' class that their utilitarian design influenced the next group of ships built for Elder Dempster. These were from the pencil of George Hunter who joined the company in 1954 as its Principal Naval Architect. The lead ship of the first batch of six ships was the *Daru* built by Scotts in 1958. She had a deadweight capacity of 9,970 tonnes on a loaded draught of 27 feet. There were three hatches forward and two aft. The four deep tanks had a new feature - they were separated by cofferdams thus enabling heated and unheated vegetable oil cargoes to be carried in adjacent tanks. The oil could be heated by re-circulating it through the engine room, a concept that had been pioneered on the *Egori* (8,331/1957). The main tank capacity totalled 1,300 tonnes and there were also two wing tanks under the midships accommodation block in the 'tween deck used for the carriage of glycerine. The cargo handling gear was heavily scantlinged and included one jumbo derrick of 50-tonnes lifting capacity at number 2 hatch.

The *Daru* pioneered one feature that was an immediate success: the midships accommodation was air conditioned. On almost all of the West African seaboard, from Dakar to Matadi, the ambient temperature was seldom less than 75 degrees F (26 degrees C) and the humidity rarely below 80%. Straight away the results were apparent: because those berthed amidships got a quiet and comfortable night's sleep

The Scotts-built Deido, second of the later batch of D class ships, photographed in original condition in 1965. See page 204 for a later view. *[Ships in Focus]*

the ship's efficiency was enhanced and these individuals were in better health. Elder Dempster did not stint on the quality of the specification for the central air conditioning plant and this paid off with trouble-free performance.

The *Degema* and the *Dixcove* followed from William Gray and those who manned them always reckoned that they had been built down to a price. Well into her service the *Degema's* cargo gear at number 4 hatch was modified to become a type of slewing derrick, but it cannot have been regarded as a success as the feature was never repeated.

The *Dunkwa* lead the trio of the second batch and came from Scotts in 1960. The Doxford engines of the second batch were turbo charged, following the example of the *Egori*. At 17 tonnes per day their fuel consumption was better by one tonne than that of the earlier trio.

Once again the company introduced a new feature in the form of a permanent swimming pool on the after end of the boat deck. On a route where attractions ashore were limited, expensive and often downright unhealthy, the facility of a pool onboard and air-conditioned public rooms enhanced the capability of the ship to generate its own social life. Elder Dempster cannot claim that the *Dunkwa* was the first British cargo ship to have a built-in pool: that distinction probably goes to Edmund Watts' *Weybridge* (Barclay Curle, 9,221/1958) but this was something of an afterthought incorporated into a forward mast house. Bibby's *Shropshire* (Fairfield, 7,244/1959) like the *Dunkwa* had hers on the boat deck and not in a working area.

The last of the class, *Dumurra*, had originally been ordered from Cammell Laird. There was some sort of a jinx across the Mersey between the local yard and the two owners head quartered in India Buildings. Despite the attraction of being able to look out of the office windows at a ship for the fleet growing on a builder's berth, Blue Funnel's order from Cammell Laird for two of the *Peleus* class had ended in inter-company anguish. Elder Dempster had only ever had the mailboat *Abosso* of 1935 built at Birkenhead at a time in their history when they were emerging from the dire days of the Kylsant crash when they were lucky to get anyone to build for them.

By 1959 Cammell Laird had become synonymous with industrial disputes often centred on demarcation as trivial as to who puts screws into a bulkhead. After a series of delays, postponed completion dates and an order never signed, John H. Joyce had enough and to the *Aureol's* builders went the order for the last of the class to come from Alexander Stephen. It was said in whispered conversations in India Buildings that the price for the *Dumurra* was not agreed until after the day of launch in March 1961 when John H. Joyce went into conclave with Sir Murray Stephen who was the third generation of the family to run the yard. At that time it was not a buyers' market and the Elder Dempster Chairman had reason to have a resultant attack of bad indigestion such was the expensive price of switching the order but the company received outstandingly the best finished cargo ship of the fleet: it was all too apparent as soon as you stepped on to the ship's accommodation gangway.

The Henderson 'D's
Concurrent with the Elder Dempster 'D's Lithgows were producing their version for Henderson's British and Burmese subsidiary. By the time the trio were delivered in 1960 and 1961 the economy of Burma was in terminal decline and the class was probably never intended to go east, hence their West African names. The substitutes for the mighty Irrawaddy were the oil rivers of the Niger Delta. Successors to the economy 'K' class, the Henderson 'D's lacked the thought-through style which Elder Dempster put into their 'D' class. However, the Henderson 'D's had a larger deadweight at 10,550 tonnes and it could be said that Borland Brothers, Henderson's partners based in Glasgow, got one up on their ultimate owner in Liverpool, as these ships served until 1981 - well into the Ocean Group era and by when all the Elder Dempster 'O's and 'D's had been sold.

With the delivery of the *Dumurra* in late 1961, Elder Dempster as an independent company had reached the high water mark of prosperity and influence. Thanks to a dedicated management team and an appreciated sea staff their story had become one of achievement in and service to a most difficult trade route.

To be concluded.

ONITSHA

Harland and Wolff Ltd, Belfast, 1952; 5,802g, 449 feet
Burmeister & Wain-type 5-cyl 2SCSA oil engine by Harland and Wolff Ltd., Belfast

Onitsha was launched on 29th January 1952 by Miss Susan Tod, daughter of Sir Alan Tod who was Chairman of Liner Holdings, the 'parent' company of Elder Dempster. In the top photograph on the Mersey she has a topmast to the main mast and a short radar mast on the bridge. The topmast was later repositioned on the bridge, as in the middle photograph from 1970.

Sold in May 1972, new owners as *Amvourgon* were officially the Cisne Compania Naviera S.A. of Panama, but ultimate owner was George Dracopoulos who traded as Empros Lines Shipping Company Special S.A. A devotee of former British cargo liners, he also ordered several SD14s. His ships were typically well kept, as the bottom photograph of a recently-repainted *Amvourgon* under the Greek flag shows, but she came to a sticky end. On 8th January 1973 she was on a voyage from Quebec to Baltimore when an engine room fire forced her crew to abandon her near Cape Gaspé. Salvors had other ideas, however, and she was taken in tow and arrived at Halifax on 11th January. Fit only for scrap, on 7th May she left Halifax on tow for breakers in Santander. *[B. and A. Feilden/J. and M. Clarkson; Fotoship/J. and M. Clarkson; World Ship Society Ltd.]*

OBUASI

Harland and Wolff Ltd, Belfast, 1952; 5,883g, 450 feet
Burmeister & Wain-type 5-cyl 2SCSA oil engine by Harland and Wolff Ltd., Belfast

Externally, the cadet ship *Obuasi* was identical to *Onitsha* apart from her heavy lift derrick, which was rated at 50 tonnes. Her post-Elder Dempster career was even shorter than that of *Onitsha*. She was photographed in Swansea during September 1963.

    Onitsha was sold in 1972 to Anglo-Pacific S.A., part of Anglo-Eastern Shipping Co. Ltd. of Hong Kong, placed under the currently-fashionable Somali flag, and renamed *Amoy*. On 9th August 1972 *Amoy* was wrecked at the mouth of the Irrawaddy River, Burma whilst bound from Calcutta to Rangoon in ballast. *[Fotoship/J. and M. Clarkson]*

OWERRI

Harland and Wolff Ltd, Belfast, 1954; 6,240g, 450 feet
Burmeister & Wain-type 5-cyl 2SCSA oil engine by Harland and Wolff Ltd., Belfast

On 14th October 1954 Mrs John Cadbury named *Owerri* after a town in eastern Nigeria. Last of the first batch of 'O's, the middle photograph from 1969 shows the signal mast in the modified position carried by the class in later life. Note also the cargo of logs on four of her hatches. The nest of ventilators on the forecastle is well seen in this view.

    July 1972 saw *Owerri* sold to Maldives Shipping Ltd. as *Maldive Courage*, as seen in the bottom photograph. Once again, she looks quite smart with her white hull ribbon, forecastle and poop. Under this name she lasted until 28th March 1983 when breakers Ali and Co. took delivery of her at Gadani Beach, setting to work immediately and completing her demolition in April. *[Ships in Focus; Airfoto (Malacca)/Roy Fenton collection]*

OTI

Harland and Wolff Ltd, Belfast, 1955; 5,485g, 450 feet
Burmeister & Wain-type 5-cyl 2SCSA oil engine by Harland and Wolff Ltd., Belfast

Oti was launched on 13th December 1955 by Ann, daughter of Elder Dempster executive Albert Muirhead, and named after a tributary of the Volta River. As noted in the text, elimination of passenger accommodation reduced the superstructure height by one deck compared with earlier O class vessels. The first two photographs show that she too underwent alteration in the position of her signal mast, relocated from the main mast to the bridge, and that she lost her white forecastle and poop. The aerial view also shows a substantial deck cargo of logs.

The third photograph, taken in Birkenhead on 15th September 1968, is intriguing in showing *Oti* with a black funnel. This may denote a voyage for Guinea Gulf, but if so, why was she in Birkenhead? It might just be relevant that, according to Cowden and Duffy, the previous October *Oti* had been briefly transferred for a Blue Funnel voyage which never materialized.

Oti was sold in May 1972 to Methenitis Brothers of Piraeus who renamed her *Mimi Methenitis*. Further sales saw her become *Goldbeach* in 1976 and *Nicolas K* in 1977, before she arrived at Kaohsiung to be broken up late in December 1979. *[Roy Fenton collection; J. and M. Clarkson; Roy Fenton]*

ONDO
Harland and Wolff Ltd, Belfast, 1956;
5,435g, 450 feet
Burmeister & Wain-type 5-cyl 2SCSA
oil engine by Harland and Wolff Ltd.,
Belfast
Sponsor of *Ondo* at her launch on 7th
June 1956 was the wife of Mr. (later Sir)
Clifford Dove, Chairman of the Mersey
Docks and Harbour Board, who named
the ship after a province of Nigeria. The
upper photograph of *Ondo* carrying a
substantial barge on deck was taken on
the New Watereway; that below in the
Thames Estuary on a particularly bright
13th January 1959.

As discussed in the text, on
6th December 1961 *Ondo* became
Elder Dempster's only serious post-war
casualty when she ran aground after
stopping her engines in order to try to
save a pilot vessel's crew. At least three
salvage companies attempted to refloat
her but in vain, and her wreck remains
visible on the approach to the River
Elbe. *[Both: Ships in Focus]*

DARU

Scotts' Shipbuilding and Engineering Co. Ltd., Greenock, 1958; 6,340gt, 460 feet
5-cyl. 2SCSA Doxford-type oil engine by Scotts' Shipbuilding and Engineering Co. Ltd., Greenock

On 10th April 1958 Mrs M. Harrison named the first of the 'D' class after a district of Sierra Leone.

In November 1965 *Daru* was given the Henderson name *Yoma* but the intended voyage to Burma was cancelled, and she reverted to *Daru*. However, her Elder Dempster name was retained when she transferred to Guinea Gulf Line services in February 1966.

Sale in April 1979 saw her become *Lone Eagle*, a name which points to ownership in the USA and, although her owner had a brass plate in Monrovia and the ship flew the Panama flag, she was indeed controlled from Houston, Texas. She was later photographed at Singapore as *Anjo One* (middle), a name she took in 1980 for owners Venture Company Inc. of Panama, a company believed to have been controlled from the United Arab Emirates. Note how the main topmast has migrated to the top of her bridge. *Anjo One* arrived at Karachi 14th February 1982 to be broken up, although work did not start until September. *[J. and M. Clarkson; R.J. Kittle]*

DEGEMA

William Gray and Co. Ltd., Hartlepool, 1959; 5,905g, 460 feet
5-cyl. 2SCSA Doxford-type oil engine by Central Marine Engine Works, Hartlepool

Named after a town in the Niger Delta, *Degema* was launched on 27th November 1958 by Mrs Gwen Arundel, wife of an Elder Dempster director. The photograph above was taken at Mid-Barrow, Thames Estuary, on 17th April 1959.

In February 1979 *Degema* was sold to a Greek gentleman named S.C. Vazeos who renamed her *Veejumbo* and put her under the Honduras flag, an interesting move as, although one of the early flags of convenience, Honduras had by now fallen from favour. In 1982 she was renamed *Dejema*, but she reverted to *Degema* for what was probably just one voyage to Gadani Beach and the breakers. *[Ships in Focus]*

DIXCOVE

William Gray and Co. Ltd., Hartlepool, 1959; 5,902g, 460 feet
5-cyl. 2SCSA Doxford-type oil engine by Central Marine Engine Works, Hartlepool

Launched on 25th March 1959 by Mrs H.R. Lane, wife of Elder Dempster Lines' Nautical Advisor, *Dixcove* took the name of a former surf port in what is now Ghana. She is reported to have been transferred to China Mutual Steam Navigation Co. Ltd. in 1972, and there is ample photographic evidence of her with a Blue Funnel, including the middle photograph by Airfoto of Malacca.

In April 1979, just over 20 years after she had been launched, *Dixcove* was sold and became *Gulf Eagle* of Gulf Shipping Lines Ltd. This polyglot organization had Pakistani principals, a management office in Hong Kong, and a head office in London. Despite this, *Gulf Eagle* remained registered in Liverpool until she was broken up at Chittagong in June 1983. *[J. and M. Clarkson; Airfoto (Malacca)/J. and M. Clarkson]*

DUNKWA

Scotts' Shipbuilding and Engineering Co. Ltd., Greenock, 1960; 6,109gt, 460 feet
4-cyl. 2SCSA Doxford-type oil engine by Scotts' Shipbuilding and Engineering Co. Ltd., Greenock

Mrs John Baring sponsored *Dunkwa* at her launch on 10th January 1960, naming her after a town in Ghana. She seems to have been little modified during almost 21 years of Elder Dempster service.

In January 1981, very soon after becoming *Clare* for the eponymous Clare Shipping Corporation, principal D. Diamantides, she was on a voyage to Rio de Janeiro when damage was sustained to her machinery, which was the first turbocharged version of the Doxford four-cylinder engine. This led to her being declared a compromised total loss, but she was bought and renamed *Resolve*. There is little evidence of her being repaired and returned to service, however, and in March 1983 she was delivered to breakers at Gadani Beach. *[J. and M. Clarkson]*

DEIDO

Scotts' Shipbuilding and Engineering Co. Ltd., Greenock, 1961; 6,109gt, 460 feet
4-cyl. 2SCSA Doxford-type oil engine by Scotts' Shipbuilding and Engineering Co. Ltd., Greenock
Deido was launched on 1st February 1961 by Mrs Dorothy Evelyn, daughter of director Malcolm Glasier. Like other members of the class, there were few modifications made to *Deido* during her Elder Dempster career. The black of her hull in the photograph on page 197 was relieved by painting the forecastle and poop white and her original signal mast was replaced with something more substantial. Both changes are apparent in the above photograph taken on the Thames in October 1978.

Deido was sold in January 1979 to Canopus Shipping S.A. and renamed *San Georgio III* under the Panama flag. In 1980 the principals, Andreas and George Kyrtatas, decided to transfer her to the Greek flag, and accordingly her saint's name was now rendered as *Agios Georgios III*. In 1982 she was laid up at Piraeus apparently remaining there until shortly before October 1986 when she arrived at Aliaga for demolition. *[Ships in Focus]*

DUMURRA

Alexander Stephen and Sons Ltd., Linthouse, Glasgow, 1961; 6,150g, 460 feet
4-cyl. 2SCSA Doxford-type oil engine by Hawthorn Leslie (Engineering) Ltd., Newcastle-upon-Tyne.
On 16th March 1961 director's wife Anne Robertson launched *Dumurra*, the only one of the class to come from Linthouse, following the cancellation of an order at Birkenhead. Once again, modifications during her time with Elder Dempster were confined to a new and stouter signal mast and the painting of her masts in a darker colour (second photo) - possibly due to the influence of Holts?. Changes following her June 1980 sale appear to have been minimal, too, and her name was simply amended to *Fumurra* and she was transferred to the fledgling Isle of Man registry. The upper photograph on the opposite page shows her under this name in August 1981, now with a narrow black top to her funnel and a less-than-pristine hull. The name of her owners, Fumurra Ltd., could not have been more opaque, but she does seem to have been genuinely owned in the Isle of Man. She was sold to breakers in May 1983 and cut up at Gadani Beach. *[Ships in Focus; Fotoship/J. and M. Clarkson; J. and M. Clarkson]*

DONGA
Lithgows Ltd., Port Glasgow, 1960;
6,559g, 465 feet
Burmeister & Wain-type 4-cyl. 2SCSA
oil engine by J.G. Kincaid and Co. Ltd.,
Greenock.
Taking its name from a river and
township in Benue Province, Nigeria,
Donga was launched on 12th April 1960
by Mrs Margaret Hodges, wife of the
Assistant Manager of Elder Dempster.
Despite this, official owners were the
British and Burmese Steam Navigation
Co. Ltd. and managers P. Henderson
and Co., and she was officially bareboat
chartered to Elder Dempster until 1964
when this concern purchased her. The
photograph was taken in the Mersey on
8th September 1977.

When sold in March 1981, her
initial purchaser was D. Diamantides
who also bought *Dunkwa*, and who
renamed her *Diamant Merchant*. In
1983 she became *Lydra*, but sale
to Karachi breakers followed fairly
quickly and by October she was being
demolished. *[J. and M. Clarkson]*

DUMBAIA

Lithgows Ltd., Port Glasgow, 1960; 6,558g, 465 feet Burmeister & Wain-type 4-cyl. 2SCSA oil engine by J.G. Kincaid and Co. Ltd., Greenock.
Launched on 8th August 1960 by the wife of Elder Dempster director Simon Cotton, *Dumbaia* was again initially chartered to the company. The upper photograph dates from 1961. As comparison with the lower photograph shows, modifications again included changes to paintwork and the addition of a much taller signal mast on the bridge.

Dumbaia was the only ship of those covered in this part of the article not to carry a further name. Sale in March 1981 saw her pass to an Isle of Man company, Questnorth Ltd., with the same principal as owned the *Fumurra*. She was soon laid up at Piraeus and still as *Dumbaia* arrived at Shanghai for demolition in April 1984. *[Both: J. and M. Clarkson.]*

DALLA

Lithgows Ltd., Port Glasgow, 1961; 6,564g, 465 feet Burmeister & Wain-type 4-cyl. 2SCSA oil engine by J.G. Kincaid and Co. Ltd., Greenock.
Launched on 1st February 1961, *Dalla* followed a similar pattern of official ownership changes and modifications as her two predecessors. Seen in the lower middle photograph when new in 1961, the bottom photograph depicts her with a tall signal mast, white forecastle and poop, and dark masts.

Her post-Elder Dempster career was short but eventful. Renamed *Marmaras* in March 1980 by D. Diamantides,, in October 1981 she first suffered the collapse of a deck in number 4 hold under the weight of a steel cargo, requiring her to divert to Rotterdam during her voyage from Rostock to Alexandria. This damage was the reason for her being laid up in Greece, but a further sale followed although without name change. A fire in September 1983 damaged her engine room and accommodation so badly that scrapping was inevitable, and in June 1984 she arrived at Split for Brodospas to do their worst. *[J. and M. Clarkson; World Ship Society Ltd.]*

Book List
48

SHIPS IN FOCUS
John & Marion Clarkson
18, Franklands, Longton, Preston PR4 5PD
Phone 01772 612855

Book List
48

A selected range of maritime books from quality publishers economical postal charges secure packing prompt service. Payment must accompany all orders and from overseas must be in Sterling with cheques payable to Ships in Focus. Remittances can be made by Maestro, Switch, Mastercard, Visa/Delta. We require card number, valid from and expiry dates, last 3 figures of security code, issue number on Maestro cards and customer's name as on card. Orders accepted by phone if payment by credit card. Postage: UK orders up to £20 add £2.00, £20-£50 add £3.50, over £50.00 free. Overseas orders by seamail: Europe/North America 10% of total cost of books, elsewhere 15%, both with a minimum of £4.50. Airmail at cost.

New from Ships in Focus Publications
CRESCENT SHIPPING
by K.S. Garrett
Includes London & Rochester, Bowker & King, Offshore Marine and more.

Coasters, sailing and motor barges, tugs, tankers, ORSVs and ferries –all part of the story of Crescent Shipping. In this book the well-known author of books on South Eastern shipping traces the origins of Crescent in the Gill family's Medway barge owning and building which began in 1849. He relates how this grew to be the major barge- and coaster-owner, London and Rochester Trading Co. Ltd., and how it expanded to form the successful Offshore Marine Ltd. As part of the larger Hays Wharf group, tanker operator Bowker & King came into the story and, after the name Crescent Shipping was adopted, diverse vessels were managed, including ferries, ro-ros, and more coasters. The story is taken up to 2008 when the company and its fleet lost its identity in the Danish Clipper group.

All these activities are covered in the 60 pages of history, which is followed by full details of all vessels owned, built, managed or otherwise associated with Crescent – a total of 650 entries. The powered vessels are almost all illustrated, many in colour, as well as a selection of the sailing craft.

'Crescent Shipping' is important contribution to the history of both British shipping and the waterborne trade of the Thames and Medway, where this successful and diverse company originated.
248-pages A4 hardback illustrated in colour and black and white £35.00

A major history of an important coastal ship owner
WILLIAM ROBERTSON and the GEM LINE
Roy Fenton and Philip Robertson

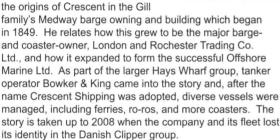

For over 120 years, the fleet of William Robertson was a major force in coastal tramp shipping. With up to fifty ships in its fleet, it was for many years the most important operator on the British West Coast. Although it lost its independence in the 1970s, echoes of it remained into the 21st century with 'gem' names in the Stephenson Clarke fleet, and many people remember the company with affection. This book does the company's history full justice, covering its ships, their trades, the Robertson family, reminiscences of employees, its involvement with quarrying, and also considers its performance as a business. But the ships, all named after gems or minerals, are the stars of the book. All 107 steamers, 26 motor coasters, 13 sailing ships and 21 managed vessels are fully detailed, and wherever possible illustrated, many at different stages of their careers. Amongst the many photos are some unique images from the company's archives showing casualties, launches and other occasions. There are also eight pages in colour. Altogether, this is a book any coaster enthusiast will relish. 144pp A4 h/b £21.00

THE BLUE FUNNEL LEGEND A History of the Ocean Steam Ship Company, 1865-1973 by Malcolm Falkus published 1990, illustrated, new copies h/b 412pp £30.00
THE TRADE MAKERS: ELDER DEMPSTER IN WEST AFRICA 1852-1972, 1973-1989 Peter N Davies 2nd edition published 2000 – new copies illustrated s/b 556pp £27.50

SHIPS IN FOCUS RECORD 48

Elder Dempster Pt 2, Everards Capable, Hobart photographers, Clipper Reefers Pt 2, Prince Line mystery, Scottish steam coasters, Railway steamers serving France plus our usual features and index for records 45 to 48. s/b 72pp (20 in colour) £7.50

Books at discounted prices see pages 2, 7 and 8.

THE MARITIME ART OF K D SHOESMITH Glyn L Evans the elusive artist and his work illustrated mainly in colour h/b 96pp £30.00

LINJER RUNDT JORDEN
Historien om Norsk Linjefart Dag Bakka Jr. History of Norwegian cargo liner services, Norwegian language throughout but excellent photos both colour and black and white h/b 320pp £25.00

DANSKE REDERIER No 10
Hojlund family (Stevns and Nordane Shipping) Bent Mikkelsen illustrated 256pp h/b £29.50

THREE NEW TITLES FROM GREECE:
LIBERTY SUCCESSORS Georgios M Foustanos well illustrated 240pp h/b £91.00
DRY CARGO SHIPS BUILT FOR GREEKS 1949-1967 Georgios M Foustanos very well illus 336pp h/b £95.00
FAMAGUSTA The Rise and Fall of a Ship's Registry 1964-1974 Georgios M Foustanos well illus mainly three per page h/b 384pp £99.00

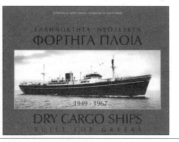

A TASMAN TRIO - WANGANELLA – AWATEA – MONOWAI -Andrew Bell and Murray Robinson

'A Tasman Trio: Wanganella – Awatea – Monowai' brings to life the fascinating lives of the three best-remembered passenger liners that linked Australia and New Zealand in the golden era of sea travel. It recalls sunlit promenade decks, cocktails in the first class lounge, invitations to the captain's table, tennis on the sports deck, dining saloons with the finest haute cuisine, cruising the Fiordland sounds, streamers and the cry of 'All ashore!' on sailing day. The story of these three ships through the exigencies of war and the uncertainties of peace is told with the help of a wealth of photos, many never before published, sourced from major collections in New Zealand and around the world. A New Zealander, Murray Robinson lives on the Kapiti Coast north of Wellington. His art is featured on the book's endpapers. This 104 page A4 hardback includes 189 black and white photos plus two maps, deck plans and paintings in colour £18.50 *For Australia and New Zealand orders please contact co-author Murray Robinson on 04 905 2428*

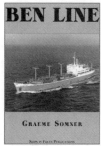

BEN LINE Graeme Somner One of Scotland's premier cargo liner companies is the subject of our latest book, written by the acknowledged expert on the company. 'Ben Line' includes the full story of the company, which sold its last ship about 15 years ago, and all its ships are fully detailed. Although best known for its sleek cargo liners – once known as the Leith yachts' – the company has also owned or managed bulk carriers, drill ships and rigs, container ships, and chemical and crude tankers, and all are included. This 232 page A4 book has a profusion of photographs and illustrations, in colour and black and white, many of which have not been published before. £28.50

BRITISH SHIPPING FLEETS 1: Manchester Liners - Fishers of Newry - J.T.Rennie - The Carron Company - Cardiff Hall Line - Runciman (London) Ltd 192pp A4 £24.00

BRITISH SHIPPING FLEETS 2: United Baltic Corporation Ltd., Chellew Navigation Co. Ltd., Thomas Dunlop and Sons, Glover Brothers, Howdens of Larne h/b 192pp £27.00. Copies of the first volume in the series, **British Shipping Fleets 1** (made up of:

Manchester Liners, Fishers of Newry, J.T.Rennie, The Carron Company, Cardiff Hall Line and Runciman (London) Ltd,) are available at the bargain price of £12.00 post free when bought with a copy of **British Shipping Fleets 2**

CLAN LINE Illustrated Fleet History John Clarkson Roy Fenton Archie Munro Now available: *Clan Line: Illustrated Fleet History* will bring together the largest selection of Clan Line photographs ever published, together with highly detailed captions and commentaries plus a fleet list researched mainly from primary sources. What is expected to be the definitive history of the ships of

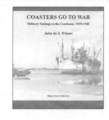

Clan Line also includes the fleets taken over in 1919 from Houston and Scottish Shire Lines, and ships acquired and put in Clan colours in the latter years of the company. This is much more than a photograph album, as there are narratives on each phase of the Clan Line story, offering many new insights into how the Cayzers built up one of the great British cargo liner companies. A4 Hardback 344 pages £34.00

COASTERS GO TO WAR - Military sailings to the Continent, 1939-1945 John de S. Winser. The part played by coasters in the Second World War was vital and perhaps little appreciated. In the first days of war in 1939, a dozen coasters were requisitioned to carry ammunition and petrol to the British Expeditionary Force in France. By June 1940, this fleet had grown to over 160, their supply task being overtaken by the urgency of rescuing troops from Dunkirk westwards as far as the Bay of Biscay. Often under fire, coasters evacuated 40,000 personnel and their story is told in Part I. Part II highlights the unique contribution coasters made to the military campaign, starting with D-Day in June 1944, when they formed part of the assault fleet, landing cargo and troops on the Normandy beaches. The book details the convoys, cargoes and challenges during an operation involving 460 coasters, of ten different nationalities. Their assignments continued until the war's end, carrying cargo to a range of continental ports, some so small that only coasters could enter them. This book documents for the first time the vital role of coasters in supporting military operations in western Europe during the Second World War. Illustrated h/b 144pp £21.00

GLEN & SHIRE LINES Malcolm Cooper-Bill Laxon-Bill Harvey History of the two lines with fleet lists covering all owned and managed vessels totalling over 150 ships, over 300 photographs and including 16 pages of colour. h/b £24.00

HARRISONS OF LIVERPOOL A chronicle of ships and men 1830-2002 Graeme Cubbin Company history along with history of its men and 333 ships. A4 400-pages hundreds of illustrations £34 00

MAURETANIA: TRIUMPH AND RESURRECTION Peter Newall This unusual book celebrated the 100th anniversary of *Mauretania*, one of the of 1907, one of the most famous liners ever built. A4 136pp with 4 page fold-out A4 s/b £19.50

THE LIVERPOOL AND NORTH WALES STEAMSHIP COMPANY John Shepherd The story of the company and its ships, its predecessors and successors Year-by-year account of the company's fortunes over the post-war period from contemporary sources, and a complete fleet list. All of the company's vessels are illustrated 64 A4 pages with colour and black and white images £12.00

2

2011 SHIPWRIGHT The International Annual of Maritime History and Ship Model Making edited by John Bowen and Martin Robson illustrated in colour h/b 208pp £30.00

A CENTURY OF SAND DREDGING IN THE BRISTOL CHANNEL, Volume 1: The English Coast, Peter Gosson, s/b 160pp £16.99

AROUND THE CORNISH COAST Peter Q Treloar includes many photos of shipping interest – harbours, ships and wrecks s/b 128pp £12.99

DOCKER'S STORIES From the Second World War, Henry T Bradford. Collection of true stories, illus s/b 128pp £12.99

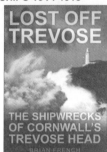

A CENTURY OF SAND DREDGING in the Bristol Channel VOLUME ONE: THE ENGLISH COAST PETER GOSSON

FLOATING PALACES – THE GREAT ATLANTIC LINERS William H Miller illus in colour and b&w 120pp £19.99

GERMAN BATTLESHIPS 1914-1918 (1) Deutschland, Nassau and Helgoland classes, Gary Staff, illustrated listings/b 48pp £9.99

GERMAN BATTLESHIPS 1914-1918 (2) Kaiser, Konig and Bayern classes, Gary Staff, illustrated listing s/b 48pp £9.99

LOST OFF TREVOSE The Shipwrecks of Cornwall's Trevose Head Brian French, illustrated s/b 128pp £12.99

MAKING WAVES A mariner's tale 1939-1948 Charles Aitchison Paddle steamer to liner, coasters to tankers – the author's varied sea career s/b 256pp £9.99

PORTS AND HARBOURS OF THE NORTH-WEST COAST Catherine Rothwell illus s/b 160pp £14.99

PORTS OF SCOTLAND 2011 30th edition many good colour photos s/b £19.00

RMS CARONIA Cunard's Green Goddess William H Miller and Brian Hawley photos artwork etc colur and black and white s/b 96pp £19.99

RUSSO-JAPANESE NAVAL WAR 1904-1905, Volume 2, Piotr Olender Battle of Tsushima, Illus with photos, diagrams and maps etc. s/b 152pp £19.99

SAILING IN STYLE DFDS Seaways Bruce Peter Photographs and advertising images h/b 128pp £18.50

SILENT WARRIORS Submarine wrecks of the United Kingdom Volume 3 (Wales and the West), Pamela Armstrong and Ron Young illustrated listing s/b 224pp £19.99

SPUTNIKS AND SPINNINGDALES A History of Pocket Trawlers Sam Henderson and Peter Drummond lists well illus s/b 160pp £16.99

THE BATTLE FOR NORWAY April – June 1940 Geirr H Haarr Events at sea during invasion of Norway in1940 illus H/B 458pp £30.00

A CENTURY OF SEA TRAVEL Personal accounts from the steamship era Chris Deakes and Tom Stanley 350 images from postcards, posters and paintings etc h/b 192pp £30.00

A HARD FOUGHT SHIP The Story of HMS Venomous Robert J Moore and John A Rodgaard story of the ship as told by officers and crew, over 170 illus s/b 362pp £19.99

A HISTORY OF THE BRITISH MERCHANT NAVY VOLUME 5 FIDDLER'S GREEN The Great Squandering : 1921-2010 Richard Woodman lightly illustrated 480pp h/b £30.00 (all earlier volumes available)

A HISTORY OF THE FALMOUTH POST OFFICE PACKET SERVICE 1689 TO 1850 The British Overseas Postal Service John Beck 320pp s/b £15.00

A MACBRAYNE MEMOIR Brian Patton a collection of memories of the company covering mainly sea but also road transport, well illus in black and white and colour s/b 282pp £15.00

A WORLD APART The Story of Hebridean Shipping Andrew Clark West Highland and Hebridean shipping through old photos 196 illustrations 112pp £16.00

ACROSS THE PACIFIC Liners from Australia and New Zealand to North America Peter Plowman illus on colour and black and white s/b 272pp £17.00

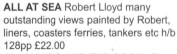

ALL AT SEA Robert Lloyd many outstanding views painted by Robert, liners, coasters ferries, tankers etc h/b 128pp £22.00

ALL HANDS AND THE COOK, The Customs and Language of the British Merchant Seaman 1875-1975 Captain Barry Thompson Terms, expressions and institutions relating to the British Merchant Navy h/b 384pp £19.50

ARCTIC APPRENTICE Rob Ellis 38 years at sea in the fishing industry and later in Merchant Navy s/b 216pp £14.95

ARTEMIS The Original Royal Princess Andrew Sassoli-Walker and Sharon Poole fully illustrated in colour – a tribute to a unique and much loved vessel s/b 120pp £19.99

BOAT TRIPS IN DEVON AND CORNWALL Ian Boyle listing of ferries etc almost all colour some historical photos s/b 112pp £12.00

BREMEN & EUROPA German Speed Queens of the Atlantic J Russell Willoughby well illus h/b 196pp £35.00

BREVERTONS NAUTICAL CURIOSITIES A Book of the Sea Terry Breverton 384pp h/b £9.99

BRITANNIA TO BEIRA AND BEYOND Mike Critchley first 5 years as an officer in RN s/b £6.00

BRITISH WARSHIPS AND AUXILIARIES 2011/12 over 80 photos in colour s/b £8.99

BUCKIE LIFEBOATS 150 Years of Gallantry Nicholas Leach history of the lifeboats and describes some rescues 64pp s/b £5.99

CANADIAN CAPERS A Seaman's Account of Intrigues and Voyages through the Corporate Jungle Svein Stokke and S C Heal the author's career at sea and ashore s/b 188pp £27.50 (imported to order)

CLYDE COAST PIERS Alistair Deayton photographic history and includes many steamers and ferries s/b 160pp £16.99

CONWAY WARSHIPS 2010 collection of well illustrated articles h/b 208pp £30.00

DANSKE REDERIER (Danish Shipping Companies) Volume 9 Lindinger, Jutlandia, Steencoasters, Bent Mikkelsen, well illus Danish/English, h/b 224pp £29.50

DEUTSCHE REEDEREIEN 38 Gert Uwe Detlefsen German language Peter Dohle, founded 1956 and have owned 350 ships+ over 1000 pictures h/b 352pp £65.00

DIE SOWJETISCHE HANDELSFLOTTE VON 1945 BIS 1991 Peter Tschursch in 10 volumes listings of Soviet merchant ships, well illustrated, reviewed in Marine news in 2007. s/b in slide binders 10 volumes £70.00 (very limited stock)

EBB AND FLOW Evacuations and landings by Merchant Ships in World War Two Roy Martin lightly illus 184pp s/b £13.99 h/b £18.99

ELDERS AND FYFFES A photographic history, Campbell McCutcheon, has now arrived on our shelves, s/b 120pp £19.99

FERRIES WEST A West Coast Photo Album A Pictorial History of British Columbia's Coastal Ferry Services S C Heal s/b 226pp £27.50

FISHING AROUND MORECAMBE BAY Mike Smylie illustrated s/b 160pp £14.99

FISHING INDUSTRY Jon Sutherland and Diane Canwell 120 photos chart Britain's fishing industry s/b 112pp £12.99

GREAT BRITISH PASSENGER SHIPS William Miller photographs, posters in both black and white and colour Edwardian splendour to present day 96pp s/b £19.99

FRERRY CRUISE ANNUAL 2011 many illustations nearly all in colour h/b 112pp £18.95

FROM OCEAN LINER TO CRUISE SHIP The Martime Art of Harley Crossley full colour 120pp h/b £35.00

INBOUND TO VANCOUVER British Columbia's Offshore Trade and Ocean Shipping Industries 1850-1945 S C Heal many photos s/b 212pp £27.50

IRELAND'S LIGHTHOUSES A photo essay by John Eagle all colour 210pp s/b £17.99

LIFE ABOARD A WARTIME LIBERTY SHIP Ian M Malcolm voyages onboard Samite, Samforth and Samnesse s/b 256pp £16.99

LIFEBOATS OF THE HUMBER Two Centuries of Gallantry Nicholas Leach history of Spurn Point lifeboats, rescues etc. 160pp s/b £16.99

LIFFEY SHIPS AND SHIPBUILDING Pat Sweeney shipbuilding and repair on the Liffey s/b 320pp £19.50

LIVERPOOL SAILING SHIPS Michael Stammers s/b 128pp £12.99

MAERSKFLADEN 1976-1990 Ole Stig Johannesen *(follow-up to Maerskbadene I and II)* h/b £46.00

MERSEY PORTS LIVERPOOL AND BIRKENHEAD Ian Collard s/b 128pp £12.99

MERSEY SHIPPING – THE TWILIGHT YEARS Ian Collard s/b 128pp £11.99

NOTHING OVER THE SIDE Examining safe crude oil tankers Ray Solly illustrated 176pp h/b 19.99

OUTBOUND FROM VANCOUVER British Columbia's Offshore Trade and Ocean Shipping Industries 1946-2006 S C Heal many photos s/b 232pp £27.50

PASSENGER TUGS AND TENDERS Nick Robbins well illustrated h/b 96pp £15.00

QUEEN VICTORIA A Photographic Journey, Chris Frame and Rachelle Cross with perspective by Captain Rynd all colour 120pp h/b £25.00

RUSSO-JAPANESE NAVAL WAR 1905, Volume 1, Piotr Olender background to the conflict and battle for Port Arthur at sea and on land. Illus with photos, diagrams and maps etc. s/b 152pp £19.99

SCHIFFAHRT IM BILD Linienfrachter volume 3 excellent photos 1 per page with captions in German 120pp s/b £14.50

SCHIFFAHRT IM BILD Tramp ships volume 3 excellent photos 1 per page with captions in German 120pp s/b £14.50

SEASPRAY AND WHISKY Tale of a Turbulent Voyage Norman Freeman story of a transatlantic voyage on a cargo vessel s/b 238pp £9.99

SECRET VICTORY Ireland and the War at Sea 1914-1918 Liam and John E Nolan s/b 320pp £19.50

SEVERN BRIDGE DISASTER 25TH OCTOBER 1960 Chris Witts collision between Arkendale H and Wastdale H illustrated 48pp s/b £4.95

SHIP KNOWLEDGE Ship design, Construction and Operation, Klaas von Dokkum 6th edition marvellous book illustrated in colour throughout h/b 384pp £60.00

SHIPS AND SHIPBUILDERS Pioneers in Design and Construction Fred M Walker, more about the characters than the ships h/b £25.00

SIETAS-TYPSCHIFF De Chronik der Trockenfrachter – the chronicle of the dry cargo ships built by J J Sietas 750 ships 1500 photos h/b 650pp £87.50

SOUTHAMPTON Gateway to the World Alastair Arnott, the relationship between Southampton and the sea, illus 160pp s/b £14.99

STILL PASSING THE POINT Bernard McCall Photo album full colour 80pp h/b £16.00

SUSSEX BEACH TRADES Sea Coal to Trippers Michael Langley photos old and modern with long captions colour and black and white h/b 160pp £18.99

THE FERRY – A Drive Through History Bruce Peter and Philip Dawson the definitive reference work: from the world's first sea-going ro-ro to the development of the jumbo ferry h/b 240pp £32.50

THE GREY WOLVES OF ERIBOLL David M Hird, surrender of German U-Boats in Northern Scotland in May 1945 144pp s/b £16.99

THE REAL PRICE OF FISH The Story of Scotland's Fishing Industry and Communities illustrated in colour and black and white 80pp s/b £6.95

TIME AND TIDE The Life of a Thames Waterman Jack Gaster 49 years work on the Thames illustrated 192pp s/b £14.99

TRAWLER DISASTERS 1946-1975 from Aberdeen, Fleetwood, Hull and Grimsby John Nicklin and Patricia O'Driscoll illustrated 192pp s/b £17.99

TUGS in Colour –Northern Europe Bernard McCall Photo album full colour 80pp h/b £16.00

US NAVY WARSHIPS AND AUXILIARIES including US Coastguard 2nd edition full colour over 100 photos s/b £9.99

---

100 JAAR WIJSMULLER Nico Ouwehand, Dutch language but many photos tugs old and new 160pp h/b £21.50

100 JAHRE LOUIS MEYER HAMBURG HAMBURG 1907-2007 Gert Uwe Detlefsen Company history and fleet list (German language) 80pp well illus h/b £14.75

A SAILOR'S SCRAPBOOK Gordon Belton his log, diary and photos taken on *Lawhill* and *Passat* 1945-1947. h/b 124pp £19.95

ADMIRALTY COASTAL SALVAGE VESSELS £22.00

AMPHIBIOUS ASSAULT From Gallipoli to the Gulf Edited by Tritan Lovering MBE Articles and accounts of landings from the sea s/b A4 landscape £35.00

ARMED MERCHANT CRUISERS Richard Osborne, H Spong and T Grover Liners pressed into services as AMC's starting with HMS Hecla 262 photos 328 pages h/b £45.00

ARMORIQUE Bruce Peter full colour throughout 96pp A4 s/b £16.00

ATHEL LINE A Fleet History Dr Ray Solly Illustrated record of their ships 256pp s/b £20.00

BALTIC FERRIES Bruce Peter examines growth of car ferries across the Baltic focussing on the development of the various owners, design and functionality h/b 128pp £18.50

BLUE FUNNEL LINE An Illustrated History Ian Collard 120pp s/b £19.99

BOMBAY TO ELWICK BAY by Bill and Sylvia Dennison exploits on the Elwick Bay along with some from WW2 148pp A5 £7.95

BP TANKERS A Group Fleet History Bill Harvey & Ray Solly Corporate history and detailed fleet history, with over 400 B&W photographs 258pp £40.00

BRAUNTON – Home of the last sailing coasters Robert D'Arcy Andrew MBE well illus with many schooner photos s/b £12.00

BRISTOL CHANNEL SHIPPING MEMORIES Andrew Wiltshire/Bernard McCall 80pp h/b £15.00

BRITANNIA'S REALM In support of the State: 1763 - 1815 Richard Woodman Vol 2 of a history of the British Merchant Navy lightly illustrated h/b 352pp £30.00

BRITISH BOX BUSINESS A History of OCL edited by Alan Bott illustrated 288pp h/b £22.50

BRITISH EXPEDITIONERY FORCE SHIPS, BEFORE, AT AND AFTER DUNKIRK by J de S Winser. H/b £18.00

BRITISH FIGUREHEAD AND SHIP CARVERS H/b £19.95

BRITISH INVASION FLEETS The Mediterranean and beyond 1942-1945 by John de S Winser 157 photos etc s/b £25.00

BRITISH STEAM TUGS H/b £24.95

BRITTANY FERRIES 1973-2007 Miles Cowsill Company history many photos mainly colour h/b 128pp £18.50

BROWNS FLAGS & FUNNELS – Shipping Companies of the World compiled by J L Loughran, H/b £25.00

BUILT BY NOBLES OF GIRVAN Sam Henderson and Peter Drummond account of one of Scotland's finest builders of fishing vessels, well illustrated and with yard list s/b 160pp £16.99

CAREDIGION SHIPWRECKS Tales of great courage and shameful behaviour, W Troughton, lightly illustrated. s/b 104pp £9.50

CARGO LINERS An Illustrated History, Ambrose Greenway very well illustrated h/b 176pp £30.00

CASTLE CLASS CORVETTES An account of the Service of the Ships and of their Ship's companies Norman Goodwin/Steve Bush h/b 530pp £30.00

CHARLES DIXON and the Golden Age of Marine painting, Stuart Boyd well illus all colour h/b 144pp £29.99

CLYDE RIVER & OTHER STEAMERS Duckworth & Langmuir Hb £25.00

CMA CGM FROM 1978 TO 2009 Marc Otini 600 colour photos, details of 700 ships French text 126pp £37.50

COAST TO COAST The Great Australian Coastal Liners Peter Plowman illustrated A4 s/b 186pp £12.99

COASTAL VESSELS A colour portfolio David L Williams and Richard de Kerbrech 80pp £14.99

COASTERS OF CORNWALL B McCall excellent colour photos 81pp h.b £15.00

COASTERS OF SOUTH DEVON Bernard McCall 86 colour photos coasters in South Devon ports 1960's to 2007 h/b 80pp £15.00

COASTERS OF THE 1950s B McCall great collection of photos of real coasters 80pp h/b £16.00

COASTERS OF THE 1960s Bernard McCall. Full colour album h/b 80pp £16.00

COASTERS OF THE AVON AND SEVERN Bernard McCall S/b £6.50

COASTERS OF THE CHANNEL ISLANDS Dave Hocquard 80pp h/b 75 clr 12 B&W photos with detailed captions. £15.00

COASTERS OF THE KIEL CANAL Bernard McCall and Oliver Sesemann Photo album with captions in English and German h/b 80pp £15.00

COASTERS OF THE MANCHESTER SHIP CANAL B McCall 80pp full colour h/b £15.00

CONVOY RESCUE SHIPS 1940-45 S/b £12.00
COOLIE SHIPS & OIL SAILERS H/b £22.00
CRUISERS, CORSAIRS & SLAVERS H/b £35.00
CUNARDER Stephen Card Reproductions of 40 paintings. H/b £37.00
CUTTY SARK - FERREIRA J.Richardson Illus in B&W and colour 246pp h/b £25.00
DE SMIT-LLOYD STORY Anywhere, anytime anyway, Nico J Ouwehand. History in Dutch with English summary and fleet list, many excellent photos 272pp h/b £34.00
DEEP-WATER SAIL by Underhill sailing ships of the 19th / 20th centuries with many plans H/b 302pp £30.00
DEUTSCHE REEDEREIEN 30 Uwe Detlefsen Siemers, Manfred Lauterjung Erik Larsen Beluga Shipping J Johannsen h/b 204pp £40.00
DEUTSCHE REEDEREIEN 31 and 32 Uwe Detlefsen Hamburg Sud h/b total of 460pp £80.00
DEUTSCHE REEDEREIEN BAND 33 Uwe Detlefsen, Oetker, Horn, Ritscher, Tamke, Transeste and DS Tankschiffahrt 204pp h/b £45.50
DEUTSCHE REEDEREIEN BAND 34 Uwe Detlefsen fleets of Orion, Blumenthal and Brise. A4 h/b 228pp £45.00
DEUTSCHE REEDEREIEN BAND 35 Uwe Detlefsen, Rickmers, photos colour and b&w A4 h/b 320pp (more pages than normal) £65.00
DEUTSCHE REEDEREIEN BAND 37 Uwe Detlefsen Atlas Levante, Argo, Transmarin and Nibbe A4 h/b 200pp £46.00
DUNDEE PERTH & LONDON S/b £15.00
ELDERS AND FYFFES A photographic history, Campbell McCutcheon s/b £19.99
ESTUARY & RIVER FERRIES OF SOUTH WEST ENGLAND H/b £16.95
F C STRICK & COMPANY S/b £15.00
FEARLESS & INTREPID 1965-2002 by Neil well illus 160pp H/b £24.00
FERRIES OF THE ISLE OF MAN 1945 to the present day Stan Basnett many photos mainly b & w 96pp A4 £15.00
FIGUREHEADS AND SHIP CARVING Michael Stammers well illus 120pp h/b £17.99
FIVE DAYS IN GREECE The Greek Ferry Industry at a Crossroads Miles Cowsill and John Hendy well illus colour/B&W s/b 64pp £15.00
FOLLOWING THE COAST Dutch shipping over the years Willem H Moojen The changes in types of coaster 1930-2005 English text/captions well illus h/b 224pp £30.00
GALE WARNING Aerial colour photos of ships in rough seas A4 h/b 96pp £26.75
GLORY DAYS BRITISH FERRIES by David L Williams excellent photos, black and white and colour, 96pp H/b £16.99
GLORY DAYS CLYDE STEAMERS by Brian Patton many excellent photos, black and white and colour, 96pp H/b £16.99
GLORY DAYS SWAN HUNTER DL Willams and RP de Kerbrech colour and black and white photos 96pp h/b £16.99
GREEK COASTAL SERVICE 1945-1995 G M Foustanos, almost 1000 photos, a fantastic book 360pp 29 x25cm h/b £69.50
GREEK PASSENGER LINERS William H Miller In colour and b&w 96pp £19.99
HADLEY SHIPPING CO.LTD) H/b £18.00
HAIN OF ST IVES S/b £8.50
HAMBURG TUGS S/b £10.50
HELLENIC LINES Vision Unlimited The Life and Works of Pericles G Callimanopulos Georgios M Foustanos beautiful book manu illustrations 302pp h/b £79.50
HISTORY OF SHIPBUILDING AT LYTHAM S/b £10.00
HMS EAGLE 1942-1978 by Neil McCart, 158pp. h/b £18.95
HMS GLORY 1945-1961 by Neil McCart in association with the Fleet Air Arm Museum 120pp H/b £19.95
HOLLANDSCHE STOOMBOOT MAATSCHAPPIJ Willem H Moojen Volume 1 company history in Dutch with 555 illustrations h/b 272pp £29.50
HOLLANDSCHE STOOMBOOT MAATSCHAPPIJ Willem H Moojen Volume 2 the ships in Dutch with over 500 illustrations h/b 288pp £29.50
HOWARD SMITH SHIPPING Enterprise & Diversity 1854-2001 by Ian Farquhar tugs either owned or operated in partnerships after 1962 not included 168pp S/b £17.50
HUDDART PARKER A famous Australasian Shipping Company, 1876 – 1961 W.A.Laxon History and fleet list - very well illustrated 236pp s/b £23.50
IN CORAL SEAS History of the New Guinea Australia The memoirs of Martin Speyer supplemented with chapters on Chief Container Service from 1985 to 2004, A well illustrated softback, 120pp, £14.00
IRISH SEA SHIPPING Brian Patton Over 300 photos of the ships and ports from 1870's to 1970's s/b £19.99
JOSEPH CONRAD MASTER MARINER Peter Villiers Traces career from Master Mariner to master novelist s/b £14.95
KELLY'S NAVY John Kelly Ltd. Belfast, A Group Fleet History W J Harvey. WSS production A4 h/b 128pp £25.00
KENT SEAWAYS Hoys to Hovercraft Michael Langley168pp A5 h/b £16.95
LAKE BOATS The enduring vessels of the Great Lakes Greg McDonnell colour through-out 160pp £25.00
LARRINAGA LINE 1863-1974 s/b£18.00
LAURENCE DUNN'S MEDITERRANEAN SHIPPING 132pp **S/b £15.95**
LAURENCE DUNN'S THAMES SHIPPING S/b £13.95
LEANDER CLASS FRIGATES S/b £15.00
LIGHT VESSELS OF THE UNITED KINGDOM AND IRELAND 1820 TO 2006 Illustrated fleet list Philip Simons – WSS 116 pp A4 s/b £15.00
LINER Retrospective & Renaissance Philip Dawson Well illustrated with plans, posters and photographs 256pp H/b £30.00
LINERS & CRUISE SHIPS (1) Some notable smaller vessels A Cooke S/b £12.95
LINERS & CRUISE SHIPS (2) Some more notable smaller vessels A Cooke S/b £13.95
LLOYD'S WAR LOSSES THE SECOND WORLD WAR Volume 2 – British, Allied and Neutral merchant vessels, Statistics – vessels posted at Lloyds as missing or untraced – vessels seriously damaged by war causes, B A and N warships and naval craft lost, vessels lost and damaged by mines or underwater explosions since cessation of hostilities H/b ***WAS £140.00 NOW £60.00***
LOOKING BACK AT BRISTOL CHANNEL SHIPPING Andrew Wiltshire, follow up to ***Bristol Channel Shipping Memories*** h/b 80pp £16.00 (expected late April)
LOOKING BACK AT BRITISH TUGS Andrew Wiltshire 101 colour photos from classic steam tugs to Z-pellers with emphasis on early motor tugs h/b 80pp £15.00
LOOKING BACK AT CLASSIC TANKERS Andrew Wiltshire excellent selection of tanker photos from mainly 1960s and 70s 80pp h/b £16.00
LOOKING FOR THE SILVER LINING A British Family's Shipowning Century 1875-1975, Martin Barraclough, company history with fleet list, illustrated A4 h/b 350pp £25.00
MASTERS UNDER GOD Makers of Empire:1816 - 1884 Richard Woodman Vol 3 of a history of the British Merchant Navy lightly illustrated h/b 384pp £30.00
MASTING & RIGGING The Clipper Ship and Ocean Carrier spar construction and rig of 19th / 20th century sailing ships 50 full page drawings and 200 sketches. H/b 304pp £22.00
MEDITERRANEAN FERRIES Richard Seville Many photos black and white and colour 96pp A4 s/b £16.00
MILFORD HAVEN More than an Oil Port Derek E Davies and D G Davies All colour photo album with captions h/b 64pp £12.00
NAVAL ACCIDENTS Malcolm Maclean, naval losses by fire groundings collisions and other causes illus h/b 450pp £30.00
NEPTUNE'S TRIDENT Spies and Slaves: 1500 - 1807 Richard Woodman Vol 1 of a history of the British Merchant Navy lightly illustrated h/b 352pp £30.00
NEW ZEALAND MARITIME IMAGES Compiled by Emmanuel Makarios, some 300 images of New Zealand maritime scenes which include many British owned or built ships. 256pp in full colour h/b £23.50
NOURSE LINE S/b £6.50
OBDURATE TO DARING - British Fleet destroyers 1941 to 1945 by John English origins, development 113 ship histories with 170 photos h/b 216pp £33.00
OCEAN FREIGHTER FINALE Nigel Jones excellent colour photos, mainly 1 or 2 per page, good captions h/b 80pp £16.00
OCEAN LINER CHRONICLES W H Miller. 136pp s/b £16.95
OCEAN LINER ODYSSEY, 1958-1969 Theodore W.Scull S/b £10.95
OCEAN LINER TWILIGHT Steaming to Adventure 1968-1979 Theodore W Scull 128 pages many photos mainly in colour of ships with onboard views also s/b £16.00
OLD TIME STEAM COASTING H/b £17.95
ONASSIS George M Foustanos 372pp 530photos h/b £89.00
PASSAGE TO THE NORTHERN ISLES Ferry Services to Orkney and Shetland 1790-2010 Cowsill and Smith illus clr and b&w s/b 96pp £16.00
PASSENGER LINERS FRENCH STYLE William H Miller, S/b £16.95
PASSENGER LINERS IN COLOUR David L Williams and Richard de Kerbrecht 80pp 85 photos £14.99
PASSENGER LINERS SCANDINAVIAN STYLE by Bruce Peter. H/b 176 pp 214 illus incl 25 colour £27.00
PASSING THE POINT Bernard McCall colour album of photos from Battery Point, Portishead, landscape format £14.50
PICTURE HISTORY OF THE CUNARD LINE 1840-1990 by Frank O Braynard & William H Miller Jr. 134pp S/b £16.95
PORT OF LONDON AUTHORITY A Century of Service 1909-2009, Nigel Watson covers all aspects of PLA with many photos old and new, mono and colour 230pp h/b £25.00
PORTMADOG SHIPS Emrys Hughes and Aled Eames new revised edition listing with some illustrations s/b A5 512pp £18.00
QUEEN OF BERMUDA by Piers Plowman and Stephen J Card. The ship and the Furness Bermuda Line 252 photos incl 43 colour. H/b 288pp £35.00
RAILWAY SHIPS AND PACKET PORTS Richard Danielson Nostalgic look at Britain's railway owned ships and ports 136pp 245 illus h/b £26.00
REMEMBERING THE LORD WARDEN British Railways' pioneering car ferry John Hendy s/b A4 48pp £12.00
REMEMBERING THE THORESEN VIKINGS Townsend Thoresen trend setters, Cowsill & Hendy colour and black and white s/b 64pp £15.00
RENDEL'S FLOATING BRIDGES Alan Kittridge illus 144pp s/b £12.50
RESCUE AT SEA The International History of Lifesaving, Coastal Rescue Craft and Organisations by Clayton Evans H/b £35.00
RICHARD DUNSTON LTD of THORNE & HESSLE, Yorkshire Shipbuilders Mike Taylor over 200 photos 160pp s/b £12.99
RISDON BEAZLEY Marine Salvor Roy V Martin 150pp 51 b&w photos £14.99
RITSONS' BRANCH LINE s/b £16.00
ROTTERDAM EUROPOORT Vol 1 Geert Mast A pictorial review of the gateway to Europe, super-tankers, pilot boats, tugs and escort vessels, many colour photos English text h/b 180pp £30.00
ROTTERDAM EUROPOORT Vol 2 Geert Mast larger ships bulk carriers shuttle tankers etc English text h/b 180pp 475 colour photos £33.95
ROUND THE HORN BEFORE THE MAST H/b £16.00
ROWBOTHAM SHIPPING A5 S/b £16.00
ROYAL NAVY ESCORT CARRIERS Cdr David Hobbs MBE 232pp H/b £19.95
ROYAL NAVY HANDBOOK 1914-1918 D Wragg 310pp h/b £25.00
RUSSIAN SEA/RIVER SHIPS B McCall all colour photos with good captions A4 h/b 80pp £17.50
SAFMARINE H/b 160pp £24.00
SCHOONER SUNSET – the last British sailing coasters by Douglas Bennet, 190 line drawings 50 photos 224pp s/b £25.00
SEVEN SEAS NAVIGATOR - SIX STARS ON THE OCEAN – A dream cruise ship for the 21st Century by M Eliseo. h/b £32.50
SHIPS OF THE WHITE STAR LINE Richard de Kerbrech company and it's 89 ships, well illustrated h/b 19.99
SHIPWRECKS AND SALVAGE ON THE EAST AFRICAN COAST Kevin Patience Illustrated h/b 276pp £17.50
SOLENT, CREEKS, CRAFT AND CARGOES Michael Longley Photos with longish captions 160pp h/b £16.95
SOUTH WEST HARBOURS Ships and trades Michael Langley photos with long captions h/b 160pp £16.95
SOUTHAMPTON SHIPPING with Portsmouth, Poole and Weymouth Photos R.Bruce Grice Text D F Hutchings 194 Photos with 24 in colour with text describing vessels featured h/b 210pp £30.00
SPANISH CIVIL WAR BLOCKADE RUNNERS Paul Heaton 112pp h/b was £20.00 now £5.00
STANDAARSCHEPEN 1939-1945 IN DE NEDERLANDSE EN BELGISCHE KOOPVAARDIJ D Gorter and G J de Boer In two volumes A4 h/b Volume 1 – development of standard vessels in all countries before, during and after WW2 (328pp) Volume 2 lists 386 ships bought by Dutch owners and 68 by Belgian owners. (336pp) Text is in Dutch but each volume contains about 700 photographs. Each volume £32.50
STEAM COASTERS AND SHORT SEA TRADERS H/b £23.95
STEAM PACKET 175 THE OFFICIAL 175TH ANNIV. BOOK Well illus with both b&w and colour H/b 160pp £21.50
T R BROWN OF BRISTOL Captain Stephen Carter Largest barge owners, sand dredgers and foremost salvage contractors in Bristol Channel s/b 104pp 95 illus £12.50
TACKY'S TUGS W J Reynolds Ltd. of Torpoint Capt Stephen Carter. illustrated 144pp s/b £12.50
TANKERITIS Chronicle Of A Master Mariner W.E.E.Lake Life At Sea On Tankers, Illus 114PP s/b £13.90
TANKERS BUILT FOR GREEKS 1948-1965 Georgios M Foustanos similar to earlier series on dry cargo ships built for Greece h/b 382pp £89.00
THE ANDERTON BOAT LIFT by David Carden 180 pp H/b £19.95
THE ARCTIC WHALERS H/b £24.00
THE CHINA CLIPPERS H/b: £22.00
THE CLYDE SHIPPING COMPANY, GLASGOW 1815-2000 WJ Harvey and PJ Telford history/fleet list illus 208pp A4 h/b £28.00
THE ERA OF COASTAL SHIPPING IN NEW ZEALAND The Small Motor Ships by Murray Jennings, generally one page per ship with photo. 192pp H/b £19.95
THE FABULOUS INTERIORS OF THE GREAT OCEAN LINERS in Historic Photographs by William H Miller Jr. with the assistance of the Museum of the City of New York,228 photos, 146pp £13.95
THE FATAL FLAW Collision at Sea and The failure of the Rules, David Thomas, support for the Master on the bridge, collision prevention regulations and possible alternative system 232pp s/b A5 £12.00
THE FISHBOURNE CAR FERRY Portsmouth to the Isle of Wight John C H Faulkner Revised, updated and includes new photographs Technical data on all ships with recollections of those who worked on them s/b 176pp £15.99
THE ILLUSTRATED HISTORY OF CANAL AND RIVER NAVIGATIONS Edward Paget-Tomlinson History of most of our canal and river navigations. s/b 404pp 0ver 300 illustrations £24.99
THE KINGDOM OF MACBRAYNE N S Robins and D E Meek History of Scotland's famous shipping company. illus h/b £30.00
THE LAST OF THE WINDJAMMERS Vol 1 H/b: £30.00
THE LAST OF THE WINDJAMMERS Vol 2 H/b: £30.00
THE LAST STEAMERS Nick Robins Tugs, ferries and coasters, illustrated s/b some colour 96pp £13.00
THE NEW CUNARD QUEENS QM2 QV QE2 Nils Schwerdtner well illus nearly all in colour 192pp h/b £25.00
THE NITRATE BOATS S/b £12.00
THE NITRATE CLIPPERS H/b £22.00
THE PYMAN STORY –Fleet and Family History by Hogg and Appleyard – history of Pyman family Fleet list with brief information on each vessel. 109pp A5 S/b £10.00
THE RIGHT KIND OF BOY A Portrait of the British Sea Apprentice 1830-1980 by David Thomas h/b 418pp £27.50

E. & O. E

BOOKS AT REDUCED PRICES

We need the space! To reduce our stock we have decided to dispose of many books at greatly reduced prices - ranging from 20% through to 50% off their original list prices. The first selection is listed below and more will follow on Lists 49 and 50 so watch this space. If you normally pay by cheque or postal order please phone us first to check as to whether or not the titles you require are still available. The quantities available vary from one through to 5 or even 10 in a couple of instances.

Description and original price	Special price
100 JAHRE LOUIS MEYER HAMBURG HAMBURG.1907-2007 Gert Uwe Detlefsen Company history and fleet list (German language) 80pp well illus h/b £14.75	£11.80
A BRISTOL CHANNEL ALBUM Chris Collard Tugs and paddlers on the Bristol Channel and at Bristol well illustrated 128pp s/b £12.99	£10.40
A COMMODIOUS YARD William Thomas & Sons, Amlwch Bryan D Hope Shipyard history illustrated with 24 appendices yard list etc. 304pp s/b £14.50	£11.60
A MACBRAYNE ALBUM Alistair Deayton and Iain Quinn selection of photos both black and white and colour s/b 128pp £14.99	£12.00
AIRCRAFT CARRYING SHIPS OF THE ROYAL NAVY Maurice Cocker illustrated catalogue of aircraft carrying ships 1912 to 1998 well illus s/b 160pp £16.99	£13.60
AN EYE ON THE COAST The Fishing Industry from Wick to Whitby Gloria Wilson 128pp s/b well illus. £12.99	£10.40
AN ILLUMINATING EXPERIENCE Gordon Medlicott 32 years working life of a lighthouse keeper illustrated s/b 132pp £14.99	£12.00
AN ILLUSTRATED HISTORY OF CARDIFF DOCKS, Volume 2 Queen Alexandra Dock, Entrance Channel and Mountstuart Dry Docks s/b 144pp £19.99	£16.00
AN ILLUSTRATED HISTORY OF CARDIFF DOCKS, Volume 3 The Cardiff Railway Company and the Docks at War John Hutton 160pp s/b £19.99	£16.00
AN ILLUSTRATED HISTORY OF CARDIFF DOCKS, Volume 1 Bute West Dock, Bute East Dock and Roath Dock s/b 144pp £19.99	£16.00
AND THE CREW WENT TOO – THE £10 ASSISTED PASSAGE Geoff Lunn Mass migration to Commonwealth illustrated s.b 192pp £17.99	£14.40
BREEZE FOR A BARGEMAN Bob Roberts on the trials and tribulations of carrying cargo under sail by barge s/b £9.95	£7.96
BRISTOL CITY DOCKS THROUGH TIME Brian Lewis ships, buildings etc with captions 96pp £12.99	£10.40
BUILDING THE BIGGEST From Iron Ships to Cruise Liners Geoff Lunn illustrated in colour and black and white s/b 160pp £17.99	£14.40
BULK CARRIERS The Ocean Cinderellas Nick Tollerton A4 192 pages £25.00	£15.00
CAMMELL LAIRD Vol 1 Ian Collard 128pp s/b £12.99	£10.40
CAMMELL LAIRD Vol 2 –THE NAVAL SHIPS Ian Collard 128pp s/b £12.99	£10.40
CAREDIGION SHIPWRECKS Tales of great courage and shameful behaviour, W Troughton, lightly illustrated. s/b 104pp £9.50	£7.60
COASTING BARGEMASTER by Bob Roberts, life on Thames sailing barges, S/b 175pp £9.95	£7.96
COSENS OF WEYMOUTH 1848-1918 A History of the Bournemouth, Weymouth and Swanage Paddle Steamers Richard Clammer History of the company's first 70 yrs. £29.95	£24.00

Description and original price	Special price
DISASTERS ON THE SEVERN by Chris Witts shipping tradgedies but land and air also 160pp s/b £12.99	£10.40
DREADNOUGHTS A Photographic History Roger D Thomas and Brian Patterson updated version includes rare and previously unpublished pictures s/b 193pp £14.99	£12.00
FALMOUTH HAVEN The Maritime History of a great West Country Port, D G Wilson Mills, Shipwrights, Shipyards and Sailors, illustrated 160pp s/b £18.99	£15.20
FERRIES AROUND BRITAIN by Miles Cowsill and John Hendy, quality photos with captions. H/b 128pp 25 x 35cm £19.50	£15.00
FINNISH MARITIME INDEX 07-08 400pp many illus mostly colour and includes articles, company histories, fleet lists etc all in English s/b £23.00	£10.00
FINNISH MARITIME INDEX 08-09 well illus mainly in colour includes articles, fleet lists (Paulins and Finnlink) s/b 400pp £24.50	£10.00
FISHING AND FISHERMAN A guide for Family Historians Martin Wilcox illus 168pp s/b £12.99	£10.40
FOR THE KING'S SERVICE - RAILWAY SHIPS AT WAR A J Mullay Well illus. h/b 128pp £25.00	£15.00
GLASGOW & SOUTH WESTERN AND OTHER STEAMERS by Alistair Deayton 128pp £12.99	£10.40
GREAT LINERS AT WAR Stephen Harding Great Eastern to Queen Elizabeth 2 Illustrated s/b 320pp £17.99	£14.40
GRIMSBY, The story of the World's Greatest Fishing Port by Peter Chapman, mainly about the town but one chapter on fishing industry H/b 160pp £14.99	£10.00
GUIDING LIGHTS – The British Lightship by Anthony Lane, 176pp s/b £17.99	£14.40
HMS/HQS WELLINGTON Archie Munro The ships wartime and peacetime service A5 106pp illus h/b £15.00	£10.00
ISLE OF MAN SHIPPING The Twilight Years by Ian Collard 128pp S/b £12.99	£10.40
KINDLY FOLK AND BONNY BOATS Fishing in Scotland and the North East from the 1950's to the present day Gloria Wilson illus 128pp £12.99	£10.40
KINGS OF THE OCEANS Part 2 1957/60 by George M Foustanos many photos test in Greek and English H/b £39.00,	£30.00
KINGS OF THE OCEANS Part 3 1961/66 H/b £41.50	£28.00
KINGS OF THE OCEANS Part 6 1975-1980 A4 h/b 480pp £59.95	£40.00
KINGS OF THE OCEANS Part 7 1981-1990 George M Foustanos. 100's photos A4 h/b 356pp £75.00	£50.00
LIVERPOOL'S LAST OCEAN LINERS The Golden Age John Shepherd illus 160pp £16.99	£13.60
MANCHESTER'S SHIP CANAL THE BIG DITCH Cyril J Wood s/b 160pp £12.99	£10.40
MERSEYSIDE – THE INDIAN SUMMER Cedric Greenwood well illus with good long captions, **Volume 1** Return to Woodside – Birkenhead, the docks and ferries 128p s/b £18.99	£15.20

Description and original price	Special price
MERSEYSIDE – THE INDIAN SUMMER Cedric Greenwood well illus with good long captions, **Volume 2** return to Pier head – Wallasey Liverpool and the hinterland 144pp s/b £19.99	**£15.20**
MS EUROPA (of 1999) Andreas Dolling text in Danish and English Excellent colour photos throughout h/b 96pp 215x215mm £21.50	**£17.20**
MV BALMORAL The First 60 Years Alistair Deayton and Ian Quinn many photos colour and black and white A5 160pp £14.99	**£12.00**
NAUTICAL TRAINING SHIPS An Illustrated History Phil Carradice training ships and reformatory schools illustrated s/b 192pp £17.99	**£14.40**
NAVAL ACCIDENTS Malcolm Maclean, naval losses by fire groundings collisions and other causes illus h/b 450pp £30.00	**£24.00**
OCEAN BOULEVARD David Baboulene Story of an ocean voyage to which the author "has merely added colour, for which no extra charge is made" 320pp s/b £8.99	**£7.19**
OCEAN LINER TWILIGHT Steaming to Adventure 1968-1979 Theodore W Scull 128 pages many photos mainly in colour of ships with onboard views also s/b £16.00	**£12.80**
P&O PRINCESS The Cruise Ships Roger Cartwright well illus list of ships 96pp s/b 24.7 x 22.3 £19.99	**£16.00**
PORT OF SOUTHAMPTON Campbell McCutcheon Tempus – 160pp s/b £12.99	**£10.40**
PORTMADOG SHIPS Emrys Hughes and Aled Eames new revised edition listing with some illustrations s/b A5 512pp £18.00	**£14.40**
QE2 FORTY YEARS FAMOUS Carol Thatcher well illus. h/b 256pp £25.00	**£20.00**
QUEENS OF THE TYNE Ken Smith Liners built on the Tyne s/b illus. 72pp £6.99	**£5.60**
REEFER SHIPS THE OCEAN PRINCESSES Nick Tolerton. A celebration of a century and a quarter of refrigerated transport by sea, and some of the worlds most beautiful ships – the pure reefers and fruit carriers. Many photos including 12 pages in full colour A4 h/b £27.50	**£20.00**
RIVER MEDWAY PLEASURE STEAMERS Andrew Gladwell s/b 128pp £14.99	**£12.00**
RMS LUSITANIA The Ship and Her Record Eric Sauder Tempus – 128pp £14.99	**£12.00**
RMS MAJESTIC The magic Stick Mark Chirnside In colour and b&w 96pp £19.99	**£16.00**
RMS QUEEN ELIZABETH 2 The last great liner Janette McCutcheon Tempus 96pp colour and B&W £19.99	**£16.00**
ROCK LIGHTHOUSES OF BRITAIN Christopher Nicholson construction and history of some of the most famous lighthouses well illus b&w and colour H/b 224pp £25.00	**£18.00**
SCHEEPVAART 2009 much enlarged £33.50	**£15.00**
SCHIFFAHRT IM BILD - SHIPPING IN PICTURES BALTIC FERRIES h/b 120pp 24 x 22cm £14.50	**£11.60**
SCHIFFAHRT IM BILD - SHIPPING IN PICTURES CONTAINER SHIPS (2) h/b 120pp 24 x 22cm £14.50	**£11.60**
SCHIFFAHRT IM BILD - SHIPPING IN PICTURES CONTAINER SHIPS (3) 120pp h/b 24 x 22cm £14.50	**£11.60**
SCHIFFAHRT IM BILD - SHIPPING IN PICTURES SPECIAL SHIPS,120pp h/b 24 x 22cm £14.50	**£11.60**
SCHIFFAHRT IM BILD - SHIPPING IN PICTURES TANKERS (3) 120pp h/b 24 x 22cm £14.50	**£11.60**

Description and original price	Special price
SCHIFFAHRT IM BILD - SHIPPING IN PICTURES A P MOLLER SCHIFF 120pp h/b 24 x 22cm £14.50	**£11.60**
SCHIFFAHRT IM BILD - SHIPPING IN PICTURES SCHULTE SCHIFF 120pp h/b 24 x 22cm £14.50	**£11.60**
SENTINELS OF THE WEAR The River Wear Watch Sunderland's River Police and Fire Brigade Neil W Mearns £13.50	**£7.50**
SHIPPING COMPANY COLOURS Edward Paget-Tomlinson full clr h/b £15.00	**£12.00**
SHIPPING OF THE RIVER FORTH by William F Hendrie S/b £12.99	**£10.40**
SHIPWRECKS OF THE NORTH-WEST COAST Catherine Rothwell illustrated s/b 158pp £14.99	**£12.00**
SINK THE FRENCH At war with our Ally – 1940 David Wragg h/b 242pp illus.£19.99	**£16.00**
SLEEP & DUWBOTEN 2008 £17.50	**£10.00**
SLEEP EN DUWBOTEN 2010 usual format all colour s/b 320pp £23.00	**£10.00**
SS CANBERRA William H Miller very well illus colour and b & w s/b 96pp £19.99	**£16.00**
SS LEVIATHAN America's first super-liner Brent I Holt well illustrated history 120pp s/b £19.99	**£16.00**
SS NIEUW AMSTERDAM The Darling of the Dutch, William H Miller, all colour s/b 96pp £19.99	**£16.00**
TALL SHIPS ON THE TYNE Dick Keys and Ken Smith s/b £6.99	**£5.60**
THE BIRMINGHAM CANAL NAVIG-ATIONS by Ray Shill 128pp s/b £12.99	**£10.40**
THE COCKLESHELL CANOES British Military Canoes of World War Two Quentin Rees the canoes and those who sailed them illus. s/b 320pp £19.99	**£16.00**
THE ERA OF COASTAL SHIPPING IN NEW ZEALAND The Small Motor Ships by Murray Jennings, generally one page per ship with photo. 192pp H/b £19.95	**£16.00**
THE PYMAN STORY –Fleet and Family History by Hogg and Appleyard – history of Pyman family Fleet list with brief information on each vessel. 109pp A5 S/b £10.00	**£7.50**
THE QE2 STORY Chris Frame and Rachelle Cross a well illustrated concise history of the famous ship from building berth to Dubai h/b 128pp £8.99	**£5.00**
THE MERCHANT NAVY; SHIPS AND TRAINS IN WORLD WAR II Ben Carver illus brief outline of wartime stories of 11 shipping companies A5 s/b 102pp £11.95	**£9.56**
THE WILSON LINE A Credland S/b £10.99	**£8.80**
THE WINSTON SPECIALS Archie Munro The story of the liners taken up in the summer of 1940. Many unpublished photos and chartlets are included. Size 233mm x 152mm 554 pages for only £27.50 post free.	**£22.00**
THE WORLDS MERCHANT FLEETS 1939 The particulars and wartime fates of 6000 ships, Roger Jordan illustrated h/b 624pp was £30.00 now £22.50	**£16.00**
UNDER THE RED ENSIGN British passenger liners of the 1950s and 60s William H Miller many photos120pp s/b £19.99	**£16.00**
WARSHIP 2008, 30th Anniversary edition h/b 208pp £30.00	**£24.00**
WARSHIP 2009 Antony Preston 10 well-written and illus articles with a review section h/b 208pp £30.00	**£24.00**
WHITE STAR LINE A Photographic History Janette McCutcheon Tempus s/b 250x225mm 96pp £19.99	**£16.00**

Post and packing must be added to all orders as follows;- UK orders up to £20 add £2.00, £20.01-£50 add £3.50, over £50.00 free. Overseas orders by seamail: Europe/North America 10% of total cost of books, rest of the world 15%, all with a minimum of £4.50. Airmail at cost
(07/03/2011)

RAILWAY STEAMERS SERVING FRANCE, 1878-1952

Part 1

John de S. Winser

This selection of cross-Channel passenger steamer photographs, mostly taken at continental ports, has been arranged in chronological order to highlight some of the main phases of the development of the railway-owned vessels which first sailed to and from France between 1878 and 1952. The extended captions intentionally concentrate on events affecting the careers of the ships whilst on Anglo-French commercial services, as opposed to any war duty or sailings on non-French routes.

VICTORIA 1878 (right)
Built for the London, Brighton and South Coast Railway Company by John Elder and Co., Glasgow; 534gt, 221·3 feet. C. 2-cyl. (48 and 83 x 60 inches) by John Elder and Co., Glasgow.
The 15-knot steel paddle steamer *Victoria* made an inauspicious departure from Newhaven on her maiden voyage on the 64-mile crossing to Dieppe on 29th April 1878. She went aground at the mouth of Newhaven harbour at low tide and, with her bow facing east, was unable to put back to port for five hours. With a passenger capacity of 490, her accommodation consisted of three staterooms on the main deck and four saloons, described as cabins, on the lower deck. The forward two, with 30 sofa berths for gentlemen and 24 for ladies, were designated for second-class passengers and the after two, with 50 and 32 sofa berths respectively, were for those travelling first class. The popularity of the route in 1887 seems evident from the fact that, on the Thursday before Easter, sailings from Newhaven were duplicated, with *Victoria* being augmented by the 22-year-old, 270-passenger *Bordeaux* (433/1865).

Victoria's uneventful voyage on this occasion was in marked contrast to that with 94 passengers aboard the following Wednesday, 13th April. Approaching a fogbound French coast at 04.20, *Victoria* struck the rocks half a mile from the shore and nine miles west of Dieppe, as depicted in the photograph. After initial panic amongst some Italian passengers, a lady's shawl caught in the pulley of the stern davit after passengers had boarded the first of the ship's boats: its bow plunged into the water, then overturned after two lady passengers jumped into it from the steamer's deck, with the result that only four of its occupants survived. The nearby Varengeville lifeboat, having itself nearly capsized during launching, found only baggage and lifebuoys but 31 passengers and six crew members aboard two of the ship's other boats, after being swept westwards along

the coast, finally reached the safety of Fecamp. On 20th April a list was issued of the names of twelve adults, three children and the ship's carpenter and boy who were drowned, unnecessarily according to one report which claimed that, as the tide was ebbing, all would have been saved had they remained on board. Although salvage was initially considered a possibility, this faded as the vessel gradually broke up against the rocks in a strong north-easterly wind. The accident might well have been avoided had the nearby foghorn been in operation but the ship struck the rocks during the 90 minutes needed to prepare fires to enable it to function.
[A.M.S. Russell collection]

VICTORIA 1886 (page 208)
Built for the London, Chatham and Dover Railway Company by the Fairfield Shipbuilding and Engineering Co. Ltd., Glasgow; 1,052gt, 309.4 feet. Compound diagonal 2-cyl. (58 and 104 x 72 inches) by the Fairfield Shipbuilding and Engineering Co. Ltd., Glasgow.
With 151 passengers on board, the paddle steamer *Victoria* made her first

outward crossing on the 21-mile route from Dover to Calais on 29th August 1886. On her return that day she attained 22 knots for short periods and, within days, was achieving a pier-to-pier time of just 66 minutes, over 20 minutes quicker than the present-day sailing schedules on this route. Operating no more than one daily round trip during her first 12 months in service, she carried nearly 20,000 passengers each way, her maximum complement being exactly 300 and her minimum seven, the latter a 13th August 1887 crossing exclusively for the Prince of Wales and party, one of a number of sailings on which royal personages were afforded exclusive use of the ship.

Navigational problems were sometimes experienced at both terminal ports. With sea breaking over Dover pier at high tide on 2nd September 1887, it was deemed unsafe for *Victoria* to berth: when conditions later improved, she was ordered to go alongside but failed to do so and it was discovered that the rough sea had carried away her after rudder. On other occasions winter storms in the Channel resulted

in the vessel being unable to enter her destination port and having to return until conditions eased. Late September 1899 saw a period of heavy swell. On the 27th, *Victoria* managed to disembark her passengers at Dover but had to move to Folkestone to land their baggage: two days later, the weather was so bad that the ship was forced to cast off at the very moment that the special train was arriving on the Dover pier.

The photograph shows the tranquil setting as *Victoria* glides bow-first into Boulogne: close examination shows the ship's stern to be bow-shaped, which, aided by bow and stern rudders, was intended to assist manoeuvring into and out of port. When the turbine screw steamer *The Queen* (featured later) was introduced in 1903, doubts were expressed in some circles as to whether the new vessel could improve on *Victoria*'s popularity, low coal consumption, easy handling and general seaworthiness. That these doubts were unfounded is clear from the fact that *Victoria* was sold for breaking up the very next year. [*A.M.S. Russell collection*]

PARIS and ROUEN 1888
Built for the London, Brighton and South Coast Railway by the Fairfield Shipbuilding and Engineering Co. Ltd., Glasgow; 804gt; 250.6 feet.
C.2-cyl. (46 and 83 by 72 inches) by Fairfield Shipbuilding and Engineering Co. Ltd., Glasgow.

SEINE 1891
Built for Chemin de Fer de l'Ouest by Forges et Chantiers de la Mediterranee, Le Havre; 808gt, 268·9 feet.
T.6-cyl. (24, 36 and 55 by 25⅝ inches) by Forges et Chantiers de la Mediterranee, Le Havre.

TAMISE 1893
Built for Chemin de Fer de l'Ouest by Forges et Chantiers de la Mediterranee, Le Havre; 953gt, 269 feet.
T.3-cyl. (23½, 35½ and 51 1/5 by 25 1/5 inches) by Forges et Chantiers de la Mediterranee, Le Havre.

MANCHE 1897

Built for Chemin de Fer de l'Ouest by Forges et Chantiers de la Mediterranean, Le Havre; 978gt, 269 feet.
T.6-cyl. (23½, 35½ and 51 1/5 by 25 1/5 inches) by Forges et Chantiers de la Mediterranean, Le Havre.

The larger ships alongside the quay in the panoramic view of part of Dieppe's Avant-Port opposite highlight the transformation of the Newhaven to Dieppe railway-owned passenger fleet from paddle to screw propulsion and from all-British to a joint Anglo-French operation. The vessel on the right is either *Paris*, which commenced sailings in July 1888, or *Rouen*, which followed her into service shortly afterwards, both of which British vessels were the last paddle steamers to be built for the route. This method of propulsion was the cause of a major incident aboard *Paris* in January 1890. She was 30 miles into her voyage from the French port when the total disablement of her starboard paddle wheel caused the ship to drift up Channel. Skilful seamanship resulted in passengers finally landing at Dover, some 60 miles east of their intended destination of Newhaven, one day later than scheduled.

Advertised journey time between London and Paris in the summer of 1898 was nine hours, using 'the commodious steamers' on the twice-daily sea connection between Newhaven and Dieppe: it was the cheapest route but not the fastest, the city-to-city time via Dover-Calais being 1¾ hours quicker.

Rouen was sold in March 1903, whereas *Paris*, after 1904 repairs

to her hull and machinery and the fitting of new boilers at Gateshead, remained in the fleet until her sale in December 1912.

The French-built *Seine*, *Tamise* and *Manche*, one of the latter two of which is seen on the left of the panoramic view, were not only the first screw-driven passenger steamers on the route but were also the first to be French-flagged. They were, however, managed by the London, Brighton and South Coast Railway, despite the British company being the junior partners in a financial arrangement based on the mileage between Dieppe and Paris being greater than that between London and Newhaven. The three French ships entered service in September 1891, December 1893 and July 1897 respectively but *Seine* was operationally the least successful of the trio. During her 11 years from 1891 to her withdrawal in 1901, *Seine* completed only 1,350 round trips, which was over 700 fewer than *Tamise* and *Manche* achieved in their first 11 years' service. Part of this can be attributed to *Seine* sustaining serious damage on 26th March 1898 in a collision with the piers on arrival at Dieppe, following which she made no Channel crossings at all in 1899; only 91 the following year and a mere 30 in 1901, her final year.

In the photograph above the open bridge of *Tamise* and the furled foresail, a standard fitting at that time to assist the ships' handling in high winds, are clearly visible as the vessel, her boat deck crammed with passengers, enters Dieppe about 1908. She and *Manche* ended their service with the introduction

of the new French vessels *Newhaven* and *Rouen* in 1911 and 1912. [A.M.S. Russell collection]

COLUMBIA and ALMA 1894 (page 210)

Built for the London and South Western Railway by J. and G. Thomson Ltd., Glasgow; 1,145gt, 270·7 feet.
T.8-cyl. (2 x 19, 2 x 29 and 4 x 31½ by 30 inches) by J. and G. Thomson Ltd., Glasgow.

Built for the 104-mile crossing to Le Havre, *Columbia* first arrived at Southampton on 19th October 1894, with *Alma* following on 10th December. The *Alma* is seen in the first photograph overleaf at the French terminal preparing for an overnight crossing to Southampton. Within the enclosed central area of the open-sided promenade deck, the ships had first-class berths for 36 passengers, while a further 78 could be accommodated amidships on the main and lower decks. Second class passengers had the choice of 50 berths, some of those in the gentlemen's saloon, situated right aft over the propellers, while the ship's plan shows a forward area of the main deck as being available 'for 33 third-class passengers or cargo'.

Both ships experienced a number of mishaps, some of which are mentioned below. In 1895, *Alma* lost her mainmast and jollyboat in a collision with the sailing vessel *Kate Thomas* (1,748/1885) on a foggy 21st March and sank the French fishing boat *Albatross* on 14th September. *Columbia* was adjudged blameless when six of the eight-man crew of the incorrectly lit fishing smack *Gazelle* drowned in a

collision off Le Havre on 12th February 1898. During *Columbia*'s cross-Channel service, fog in the Southampton area was held responsible for the steamer sustaining collision damage – to her stem against the quay on 17th September 1895; to her starboard bow in contact with the steamer *Vesuv* (912/1881), inbound from Konigsberg, on 17th February 1897 and to both bows against the anchored Leith-registered *Cholmley* (1,368/1880) on 20th October 1901. On 1st April 1902, the full-rigged barque *Cambrian Princess* (1,394/1877) went down in four minutes, drowning 11 of her crew, following a collision with *Alma*, nine miles south-east of the Isle of Wight.

By 1906, the appearance of *Columbia* had been altered during re-boiling and the middle photograph of the ship at Le Havre clearly shows that the space between her funnels has been much reduced. Both ships ended their service on being replaced by the new *Normannia* and *Hantonia* in 1912. [*A.M.S. Russell collection; Author's collection*]

DUCHESS OF YORK 1895 (opposite)
Built for the South Eastern Railway by R. and H. Green Ltd., London; 996gt, 270 feet.
Compound diagonal 3-cyl (48 and 2 x 68 by 72 inches) by John Penn and Sons Ltd., London.

PRINCESS OF WALES 1898
Built for the South Eastern Railway by Laird Brothers, Birkenhead; 1,009gt, 270 feet.
C.3-cyl. (47 and 2 x 66 by 72 inches) by Laird Brothers, Birkenhead; 740 IHP.

Duchess of York was ordered for the 25-mile Folkestone to Boulogne route, which was benefiting in 1895 from the diversion of traffic from Calais, where harbour conditions were unsatisfactory, pending improvements. Although scheduled for delivery at Folkestone firstly on 31st May, then on 15th June 1895, in fact *Duchess of York* did not carry any passengers at all either that year or the next. In a quite extraordinary and little publicised turn of events, the South Eastern Railway advised the builders that 'the vessel is of no use whatever', on the grounds of inadequate speed, unsatisfactory stability and excessive draught. The dispute went to court and, on 6th January 1896, the builders were ordered to refund the £41,712 already paid, plus interest.

That July, a survey report concluded that the main fault with the ship lay in her form beneath the water and that, if a portion of her bottom was cut out and rebuilt, the vessel would become suitable for service. The alterations were duly carried out and the elimination of 40 deadweight tons of ballast, the extra stability, improved steering and increased speed by one half knot to 18·5, during trials in May 1897, made her acceptable to the railway company, which paid £2,000 towards the work and took delivery two years later than planned.

The upper photograph opposite shows the vessel approaching her berth in Boulogne harbour, from where, on 4th November 1897, she was forced to return to Folkestone using only

her after boilers, as a result of a main steam pipe explosion. On 21st May 1898 a ship, named *Princess of Wales*, was launched, somewhat predictably at a different shipyard from her near sister and, encountering none of the problems which beset the earlier ship, passed her six-month guarantee inspection 'in a satisfactory manner'. Both steamers had distinctive bell-top funnels, which can be seen in the middle photograph of *Duchess of York* entering Boulogne at speed, but the long spoke-like openings of her paddle box were not repeated in the later vessel. The advent of the turbine screw ships in 1903 resulted in *Duchess of York*'s disposal the following year, leaving *Princess of Wales* to continue in the fleet until early 1910, being mainly employed on excursion and extra sailings during her latter years. [A.M.S. Russell collection; Author's collection]

VICTORIA 1896 (page 212)
Built for the London and South Western Railway by J. and G. Thomson, Glasgow; 709gt, 220·5 feet.
T.6-cyl. (13½, 21 and 33 by 24 inches) by J. and G. Thomson, Glasgow.

VERA 1898
Built for the London and South Western Railway by Clydebank Engineering and Shipbuilding Co. Ltd., Glasgow; 1,136gt, 270 feet.
T.8-cyl (2 x 19½, 2 x 31 and 4 x 35 by 27 inches) by Clydebank Engineering and Shipbuilding Co. Ltd., Glasgow.

Ordered in February 1896, *Victoria* made her first departure from Southampton a mere five months later, on 25th July, and commenced sailings between Jersey and France on 1st August. Though of similar design to the 1894-built steamers *Columbia* and *Alma*, *Victoria*'s smaller size and lighter draught enabled her to negotiate ports at all states of the tide. Her diminutive dimensions are immediately obvious from the photograph on page 212 taken at St Malo showing *Victoria*, on the left, astern of *Vera*: both ships were completed at the same shipbuilding yard, a fact not immediately obvious owing to a change of name in 1897.

A 19·5-knot steamer with a passenger capacity of 743, *Vera* was employed on a number of routes from Southampton but St Malo was her destination in thick fog on the evening of 15th July 1905 when she went aground near Yarmouth, Isle of Wight. Two powerful tugs were unable to move her on the morning of the 16th and it was not until that evening that she was finally able to resume her voyage.

In 1918 it was decided that the high cost of operating passenger sailings from Jersey to St Malo and Granville was no longer justified: *Victoria* therefore closed the service that September and was then put on the sale list the following February. After re-boiling and extensive repairs in 1920, *Vera* became part of the Southern Railway fleet in 1923 but made only 38 sailings in 1931. This total was increased to 228 the following year, not by her use on an aborted plan to open a Southampton to Cherbourg service but by her resuscitation of the Jersey to France service, which *Victoria* had closed 14 years earlier. Encouraged by a significant increase in tourist traffic

from France to Jersey and the prospect of an acceptable financial return, compensation was paid to the French company to withdraw their unsatisfactory service. *Vera* commenced railway ship sailings in June 1932 and the carriage of more than 28,000 passengers that year prompted the building of a new steamer, which displaced the 35-year old *Vera* in 1933. [A.M.S. Russell collection]

MABEL GRACE 1899 (below)
Built for the South Eastern and Chatham Railway by Laird Brothers, Birkenhead; 1,315gt, 300 feet.
3-cyl. (55 and 2 x 77½ by 72 inches) by Laird Brothers, Birkenhead.
The London, Chatham and Dover Railway merged with the South Eastern Railway in 1899 to form the South Eastern and Chatham Railway. Ordered by the South Eastern in preparation for a boost in traffic for the 1900 Paris Exhibition, the paddle steamer *Mabel Grace* entered the joint fleet in September 1899, the first new vessel to do so. She is seen below proceeding at speed out of Boulogne on the route to Folkestone for which she was designed. On the 12th of the following month, the ship made a special sailing from Dover taking 132 members of the Incorporated Law Society on a day excursion to Boulogne, the advertised cost of such excursions about that time being 6s.6d (about 32p).

In her first year of service, *Mabel Grace* was involved in a serious accident, resulting in the death of one man on board and injury to another. It occurred on 10th December when the paddle steamer rammed the starboard side of the engine room of the Swedish collier *Lisa* (1,577/1898), leaving the latter ship in danger of sinking, whereas *Mabel Grace*, her stem stove in, reached the safety of Folkestone before proceeding to Tilbury for repairs.

Although paddle propulsion had been replaced on other routes to France, navigation in Boulogne harbour was hampered by the restricted depth of water and, until this could be rectified, the lighter draught of paddle steamers made them better suited to serving that port. The extra dredging subsequently put in hand enabled screw ships to operate effectively and the days of the railway cross-Channel paddle steamer were consequently numbered. Although *Mabel Grace* survived a few years in support of the new ships, her end came in 1909 after only 10 years' service. [A.M.S. Russell collection]

ARUNDEL 1900
Built for the London, Brighton and South Coast Railway by William Denny and Brothers, Dumbarton; 1,067gt, 269·1 feet.
T.8-cyl. (2 x 23½, 2 x 35½ and 4 x 37½ by 27 inches) by Denny and Co., Dumbarton.
BRIGHTON 1903 (opposite top)
Built for the London, Brighton and South Coast Railway by William Denny and Brothers, Dumbarton; 1,129gt, 273·6 feet.
Three steam turbines by Parsons Marine Steam Turbine Co. Ltd., Newcastle-upon-Tyne.
Fitted with triple-expansion engines for the Newhaven to Dieppe route, *Arundel* was required to make the passage in no more than 3 hours 12 minutes and, on her trials, achieved a speed of 20·69 knots. She commenced service in July 1900 and was utilised to the maximum in

1902 and 1903, completing 290 and 307 round trips respectively.

Keen to benefit from the latest developments, the London, Brighton and South Coast Railway decided in 1902 on a new ship driven by Parsons steam turbines. Although ordered from the same builders two months before *The Queen* (see below), the new *Brighton* was not completed until after her and consequently lost out on the pioneering acclaim which greeted the Dover-based railway steamer. Delivered at Newhaven on 28th August 1903, four weeks later than planned, *Brighton* commenced passenger service that September and, on 18th November, exceeded expectations by achieving a record pier-to-pier time of 2 hours 50 minutes, at an average speed of 21·5 knots. Of similar appearance to the twin-screw *Arundel*, *Brighton* was a triple-screw vessel and is seen above as she departs from Dieppe.

Brighton's routine was very seriously interrupted in 1910, following her departure for Dieppe on an evening sailing on 5th November. She put back to Newhaven without loss of life but minus her forward funnel, mainmast and port lifeboat and with her after funnel twisted and her hull seriously damaged abaft the engine room. She had collided with the world's largest square-rigged sailing ship, the Valparaiso-bound German *Preussen* (5,081/1902), which became a total loss, unlike *Brighton* which was repaired and returned to service.

In the early hours of a foggy 24th February 1929, *Arundel* was arriving off the Newhaven breakwater from Dieppe when she sustained serious underwater bow damage by

ramming the fully-laden collier *Tamworth* (1,332/1924) inbound from Sunderland.

In October 1930, *Brighton* was sold for conversion into a private yacht whereas, after repairs, the older *Arundel* continued in service and carried 2,226 day excursionists from Brighton to Dieppe between mid-July and mid-September 1932. She was, however, displaced by the arrival of a brand new *Brighton* in 1933 and sold. *[A.M.S. Russell collection]*

THE QUEEN 1903
Built for the South Eastern and Chatham Railway by William Denny and Brothers, Dumbarton; 1,676gt, 309·9 feet.
Three steam turbines by Parsons Marine Steam Turbine Co. Ltd., Newcastle-upon-Tyne.

ONWARD 1905 (below)
Built for the South Eastern and Chatham Railway by William Denny and Brothers, Dumbarton; 1,671gt, 311·2 feet.
Three steam turbines by Denny and Co, Dumbarton.

In September 1899 the advantages of turbine propulsion for passenger vessels on cross-Channel service were publicly stressed by Charles Parsons, who pointed out that its use would reduce the weight of the engines, shafting and propellers by some 50%. To benefit from this new development, *The Queen* became the first sea-going merchant ship in the world to be delivered with turbine propulsion and was the first screw steamer to run railway passenger services across the Strait of Dover. She made her maiden commercial voyage

between Dover and Calais on 29th June 1903, having completed a crossing with invited guests two days earlier. In addition to having triple screws, her design also incorporated a stabilising device consisting of a rolling weight on rails: it was, however, discarded when tests revealed this feature to have a totally opposite effect from that intended.

The Queen was followed by four similar ships: the 4th May 1905 outward maiden crossing of the second steamer, Onward, broke the Dover to Calais speed record with a time of just 50 minutes, while the return crossing that day was noteworthy for carrying King Edward VII as a passenger. The three other ships, Invicta (1,680/1905), Victoria (1,689/1907) and Empress (1,695/1907), made their maiden

voyages between Dover and Calais on 13th July 1905, 1st May and 15th June 1907 respectively, the intention being that two ships would operate between Dover and Calais and two between Folkestone and Boulogne, while the fifth was under refit or on stand-by. Not surprisingly, this arrangement did not anticipate the Folkestone to Boulogne route being simultaneously deprived of both of its ships on 30th May 1908. During an outbound sailing with 193 passengers aboard in patchy thick fog, Onward was responsible for a head-on collision with The Queen, as a result of which a bow lookout aboard Onward was killed by flying debris. Close examination of the accompanying photograph, taken soon after the collision, shows a horizontal rip in

Onward's hull extending from her port anchor as far aft as her superstructure: a 15-foot long and 3-foot deep hole below the waterline has resulted in the ship being slightly down by the head but her integrity was preserved by the closing of all openings in the watertight bulkheads, a safety feature which could be activated from the bridge. With Onward going to Dumbarton and The Queen to London, the steamer shortage was compounded when Victoria, sent to Folkestone as a replacement, stripped a turbine blade two days later and also required repairs. In the First World War, The Queen was lost in action on 26th August 1916 and Onward caught fire and capsized at Folkestone in September 1918 but was raised, then sold. [M. Walker collection]

NEWHAVEN 1911 (left upper) and ROUEN 1912 (left lower)

Built for Chemin de Fer de l'Etat Francais by Forges et Chantiers de la Mediterranee, Le Havre; 1,656gt, 292 feet. Three steam turbines by Forges et Chantiers de la Mediterranee, Le Havre. Although the Newhaven to Dieppe route was the shortest between the two capital cities, its longer sea passage, compared with the Strait of Dover routes, meant that speed was an important factor in the competition for London to Paris passenger business and the stakes were raised with the introduction in 1911 of the French Newhaven. A triple-screw, coal-burning, turbine steamer with a capability of achieving 24 knots, she was joined by Rouen the following year. Both ships initially had a passenger capacity of 935; were equipped with sleeping berths for 240 and carried a crew of 65.

In the early hours of 5th August 1924, whilst making for Dieppe, Newhaven went aground in thick fog near Berneval Plage, nine miles east of her French terminal, as depicted in the first illustration. Passengers were landed safely, as was their luggage and three cars, but the ship resisted early attempts by four tugs to move her and it was not until the 14th that she was refloated and towed to Dieppe, having sustained damage to her bow, shell plates and engines. Damage to the passenger ships, which were at times required to leave and make port in conditions no other vessels would attempt, was accepted as part of the price of maintaining regularity on continental routes forming part of an elaborate chain of international railway connections.

The 1928 introduction on the route of the British steamer Worthing, with her superior accommodation, prompted the decision to modernise Newhaven and Rouen and the external result can be seen in the lower

photograph of the latter ship at Dieppe as a single funnelled 1,882 gross ton oil-burner, with the open-sided areas replaced by plating and windows.

On 14th May 1940 *Newhaven* arrived at Newhaven on her last ever commercial sailing from Dieppe and closed the service for over four years, *Rouen* having made the final outward sailing six days earlier. The ships were later taken over by the Germans and both returned to Dieppe from Kiel in October 1945, *Rouen* under her own steam and *Newhaven* under tow. Although *Rouen* was considered for conversion for the carriage of cargo only, it was concluded that both ships were beyond economic repair and consequently saw no post-war service. [*A.M.S. Russell collection*]

NORMANNIA (top) and HANTONIA
1912 (right)
Built for the London and South Western Railway by the Fairfield Shipbuilding and Engineering Co. Ltd., Glasgow; 1,567gt (Normannia) and 1,560gt (Hantonia), 290·3 feet.
Two sets of geared steam turbines by the Fairfield Shipbuilding and Engineering Co. Ltd., Glasgow.
In April 1911, quotations were received by the London and South Western Railway from John Brown, Cammell Laird, Denny, Fairfield and Thornycroft for two new steamers, with prices ranging from £69,000 to £86,000 per ship. Fairfield won the contract for what became the first steamers in the world to be equipped with geared turbines. Both ships were launched in 1911 with *Normannia* entering service from Southampton to Le Havre on 2nd April 1912 and her sister, *Hantonia*, starting her maiden voyage on the same route on 8th May. The civilian service

continued throughout the First World War, except for a two-week interruption from the end of March 1918, a year during which *Hantonia* was involved in two major incidents. In total darkness on 8th March, she took aboard 180 wounded from the hospital ship *Grantully Castle* (7,612/1910), sinking after colliding with a naval trawler, and on 30th April she sustained serious bow damage in contact with HMS *Teviot*. In December 1918, in appreciation of their courage and skill, testimonials were presented by the British military officers at Le Havre to the masters of both steamers. This high regard for the ships' officers was not always shared by their employers, who had retired *Normannia*'s master for improper navigation after a 31st July 1915 collision and who later reprimanded the replacement master after the ship became stranded off her French terminal on 12th December 1919. Around that time, the annual salary of a master on the Le Havre route was £240, with the prospect of a £20 bonus for exemplary service.

Unusual events included the theft from *Normannia*'s mail room on 13th September 1917 of a box containing £100 in English silver coin and, on 3rd April 1922, *Hantonia*'s scheduled departure from Southampton, despite rot having caused the upper part of her main topmast to collapse on to her main deck.

When installed, apprehension was reported in engineering circles as to whether the geared turbines would withstand the strain of continuous service. In fact, *Hantonia* was annually steaming around 27,000 miles in the early 1930s and went on to exceed her planned 25-year lifespan by nearly 60%.

The upper photograph shows *Normannia* arriving at Le Havre

about 1935: on 30th May 1940, she became a Second World War loss at Dunkerque. *Hantonia* survived and, bereft of a mainmast and never equipped with radar, was the mainstay of the overnight Le Havre service from 2nd June 1947, a service which was poorly patronised, with the ship carrying just 19 passengers on one December 1948 inbound crossing. Although advertised as a London to Paris service, French Railways declined to operate a boat train to the quayside at Le Havre in post-war years, arranging only a motor coach connection between the ship and the main railway station, thereby extending the journey time by two hours. *Hantonia* was finally replaced on 1st March 1952 and the photograph below shows the ship at Southampton, with the 1947 *Falaise*, in the background, highlighting 35 years of cross-Channel steamer development. [*Ships in Focus collection; Author's collection*]

To be concluded.

CAPABLE

K.S. Garrett

This small ship had an eventful life having been constructed during the First World War and being sunk just over twenty years later in the second conflict. She was completed in 1918 by the small Frisian shipyard of Gebroeder Zwolsman at Mist as the auxiliary schooner *Grana*. There are doubts concerning her provenance; it has been suggested that she was a speculative venture by the shipbuilder but also that she was ordered by a Norwegian owner on the basis that he would not pay in full until after the cessation of hostilities. This in itself must have been a hostage to fortune because the post-war situation would have been dictated by the victor and, at the time the order was placed, the outcome of the war was still uncertain, to say the least.

That the ship was built at all was due to the continued neutrality of the Netherlands, a small nation that had to consider her powerful neighbour and the other protagonist across the North Sea. Steel for the ship had come from Germany with the proviso that it should not be used to assist the British or French war effort. On the other hand, the British sea blockade of Germany and the extensive minefields rendered any trading in the North Sea or Baltic Sea, however innocent, extremely hazardous.

In the event the ship, although managed by a Norwegian, emerged from the shipyard wearing the Dutch flag and had a Dutch neutrality flag painted on her side. Judging by what looks like snow in the background the first photograph probably shows the ship shortly after completion during the winter of 1918 to 1919. It is not known if she actually traded like this at the time. A factor pointing to Norwegian influence from the start is the name *Grana* that translates from the Norwegian into English as 'spruce'. Perhaps it indicated the nature of the anticipated cargoes. (Absolutely no connection with Howard Hughes and his monster flying boat of the 1940s!).

Built of steel, *Grana* had joggled plating, a method of construction more common on the continent than in Great Britain and obviated the need for joggled frames or fillers. Her original engine was a

Grana during the winter of 1918-19 with Dutch neutrality markings. *[E.A. Kruidhof collection]*

two-cylinder Kromhout hot bulb oil engine made by Firma D. Goedkoop in Amsterdam. Her first owner was N.V. Scheepvaart Maatschappij Grana, Rotterdam and the manager was O.C. Sætrang & Co., of Skien, Norway. Things were moving fast and wartime restrictions were being lifted because by 1919 the manager had become the owner and the manager was now A/S Grana G.M. Grønvold of Skien, although the ship was still registered in Rotterdam. However, by April 1919 she had been sold to A/S Mercur with manager C.B. Nielsen, also both of Skien, but by this time she had been registered in Skien and was now fully Norwegian.

Near disaster struck on 25th July 1919 when, loaded with coke for Nakskov, *Grana* stranded on Halle Riff and had to be towed to her destination for discharge and repairs. On 7th August 1919, during a ballast passage from Nakskov to Haget, she was stranded and abandoned off Björnnabben on the island of Öland. She was later refloated and taken to Oskarshamn. Although it has been reported that she sailed from here to load timber at Kalmar it appears that at some stage she was declared a constructive total loss and abandoned to her underwriters. The next part of the story is rather vague but what is

Kromhout two-cylinder hot bulb oil engine. *[Marine Oil-engine Handbook]*

certain is that on 22nd March 1920 she was registered in London by Frederick Thomas Everard of Greenhithe. Who sold her to him and how she got to London will probably remain a mystery. Quite possibly she sailed to England with her cargo of Swedish timber from Kalmar without the aid of her damaged engine.

By the time she was registered in London she had probably been repaired and what has baffled some researchers is that her engine is now described as being made by Plenty and Sons of Newbury, yet is essentially the same as her original Kromhout. The explanation is that Kromhout engines were made by Plenty under license from Perman and Co. Ltd., the London agents for Goedkoop of Amsterdam. The strong possibility is that she received a complete new engine before being registered as a British ship in 1920.

Below: The Perman and Co. Ltd. store at Bermondsey. *[Kromhout catalogue]*
Top right: *Grana* at Rouen about 1924. *[G. Dines]*
Upper middle right: The crew of *Grana* with Captain Dines in the centre. The urchin on the right is an uninvited guest. *[G. Dines]*
Lower middle right: The contemporary Plenty two-cylinder oil engine. *[Plenty catalogue]*
Bottom: The Plenty four-cylinder 2SA 4P50-type oil engine. *[Plenty catalogue]*

Grana settled down to normal coastal trading and the son of one of her masters recalled summer trips with his father when the ship motored rather than sailed most of the time. Amongst other trades she was often engaged in was carrying bottles from Ipswich to Rouen. Despite the anecdotal reference to using the engine, there are at least two rather dramatic paintings of the schooner under full sail which were used on calendars and other advertising material. The use of the engine indicates that the crew were probably paid weekly wages rather than being 'on the share' when they would have had to pay a proportion of the fuel costs.

By 1924 the company, although still very much involved with sailing barges, was thinking that the future lay with powered craft. Experience had been gained with the first two *Grit*s and although both came to untimely and unfortunate ends it was

nothing to do with the engines in either case. The *Grana* must have looked like a suitable craft for conversion.

In the event it was a comprehensive conversion job. Bowsprit, mainmast and rigging were removed as was the two-cylinder Plenty/Kromhout engine. By this time Plenty was no longer making the Kromhout engines and had developed a family of main and auxiliary marine engines of its own. These early engines were remarkably similar to the Kromhout units but the company had patented several improvements that were built into the new engines. Production had started in 1920 with a single-cylinder unit designated 1P50 which was works number 501. The new four-cylinder unit was designated 4P50 and *Grana* received number 524.

A new deckhouse was erected aft with an open bridge and a tall thin funnel bearing the diagonal white and red company mark. These alterations and the change of name to *Capable* were registered on 16th April 1925 but, despite the extent of the conversion work, it was not considered necessary to re-register the vessel. In later years a proper wheelhouse was added. Her new mainmast was the lower mast taken out of the ketch *Martinet* (126/1912) when she was re-rigged.

According to *Capable's* cargo book the first cargo was loaded in London between the 11th and 15th April and consisted of 200 tons of cement and 50 pipes of wine consigned to Lowestoft and Norwich. After loading she returned to Greenhithe, presumably for late trials and adjustments, before sailing on the 19th. She arrived at Lowestoft on the 21st and Norwich on the 26th where she discharged and sailed on the 27th April. Freight money for the wine was £28-2s-6d (£28.125) and for the cement £76-1s-0d (£76.05). She then sailed across the North Sea to Boom in Belgium to load 250 tons of bricks for London at 8/- (40p) per ton. She continued to load cargoes of continental bricks for London for several months before spreading her wings and interspersing the brick cargoes with coal from Keadby to Margate, also at 8/- (40p) per ton.

In early 1926 *Capable* picked up some cargoes of cement in London consigned to Poole or ports further west before loading china clay at Par for the paper works at Snodland. Such a round trip became a regular feature of

Above: The final stages of the conversion of *Capable*. Note the compass adjuster on the open bridge. Opposite page top: The Plenty four-cylinder 2SA 4P50-type oil engine installed during the conversion. *[All: F.T. Everard and Sons Ltd. archive]*

218

her trading in later years; cement down Channel followed by china clay, stone or sand back to the Thames or Medway. Typically the freight on the two cargoes would be in the region of £220. One can pick out some occasional cargoes, for instance flints from St. Valery en Caux or Le Treport to London, a cargo that was still being carried until the company sold the little 199g 'F' class dry cargo ships in the mid 1970s.

Quite by chance a copy of a bill of lading for a coal cargo carried by *Capable* in October 1926 has survived and is reproduced overleaf. The cargo was loaded in Rotterdam for discharge at Whitstable and consigned to the Whitstable Electric Co. Ltd. Although the master, Fred Bailey, has, correctly, signed the bill claused 'quality and quantity unknown' the written description is quite specific: '252,652 kilos of Westphalian Anthracite'. The agreed freight rate was 10/- (50p) per ton yielding a gross freight of £126.25p. There is also a 'statement of facts' setting out times of arrival and departure, loading and discharging.

Another cargo worthy of mention was sand from the Cornish port of Pentewan to various destinations, mainly in the London area. This movement continued on a regular basis from 1926 until the ship was sold in 1935. The sand was used to make building blocks and was dug from the beach where there seemed to be an

The newly converted *Capable* on trials. *[F.T. Everard and Sons Ltd. archive]*

UNITED COAL COMPANY
ROTTERDAM.

Copy

Cargo.

Tons of	in	hold
„	„	„
„	„	„
„	„	„
„	„	„
„	„	„

Total _____ Tons.

Coals on board for Ship's use
independent of Cargo.

Tons in _____

Tons in Bunkers _____

Tons in Bunkers on arrival. _____

Total _____ Tons.

Leadstamps attached to

Arrived off Stook 30th Sept 4.30 pm
Arrived loading berth 2nd Oct 11 am
Commenced loading 2 Oct 1 0 pm
Finished loading 2   4.45 pm

Freight: _____

Received on account of Freight:

on which Insurance and Interest have been paid.

_____

Shipped in good order and condition
by the **UNITED COAL COMPANY, 110 Pieter de Hooghweg, Rotterdam,**
in and upon the good ~~Steamship~~ *Motor vessel* called the *Capable*
whereof is Master for this present voyage   and now
lying in the Port of *Rotterdam* and bound for *Whitstable*

(with liberty to call at any ports, in any order, to sail without Pilots, and to tow and assist vessels in distress
and to deviate for the purpose of saving life or property):

*252652 Kilos Westphalian Langenbrahm
Anthracite Nuts 20/30 m.m*

which are to be delivered in the like good order and condition at the said Port
of

The Act of God, Enemies, Restraints of Princes and Rulers, Perils of the Seas excepted. Also Fire,
Barratry of the Master and Crew, Pirates, Collisions, Strandings, and Accidents of Navigation, or latent defects
in, or accidents to, Hull and/or Machinery, and/or Boilers always excepted, even when occasioned by the
negligence, default or error in judgment of the Pilot, Master, Mariners, or other Persons employed by the
Shipowner, or for whose Acts he is responsible, not resulting however, in any case from want of due diligence
by the Owner of the Ship or by the ship's Husband or Manager.

unto *Order*

or   Assigns, he or they paying Freight for the same as per Charter-Party
dated   192 , all the terms and exceptions
contained in which Charter are herewith incorporated.

General average payable according to York-Antwerp Rules 1890.

In Witness whereof the Master of the said Ship has signed *two* Bills
of Lading, all of this tenor & date, drawn as a set, consecutively numbered, any one of
which being accomplished, the others to be void.

Dated at *Rotterdam,* the *2 October* 192*6.*
QUALITY AND WEIGHT UNKNOWN

F V Bayley

A bill of lading for a coal cargo from Rotterdam to Whitstable in late 1926. *[F.T. Everard and Sons Ltd. archive]*

endless supply. In fact, when work ceased during the war while the beach was mined and fortified the sand built up to such an extent that the port became landlocked and work did not resume. The freight for a cargo to the Thames was about 6/6d (32.5p) per ton: not a fortune but it did keep a ship earning some money on a return voyage from the West Country. Everard ships from the sailing barges to the new motor ships of 450 tons deadweight were regular visitors to Pentewan; during an eight month period between August 1934 and April 1935, of the sixteen ships involved, eleven of them were owned by the company. One elderly, retired master when asked what the attraction was in the sand, thought for a while but the only thing he could think of was that they were giving the stuff away.

Starting in February 1931 *Capable* carried several cargoes at

Capable in service: note the furled sails. *[F.T. Everard and Sons Ltd. archive]*

Capable in the Thames alongside the second *Grit* of 1923. *[F.T. Everard and Sons Ltd. archive]*

monthly intervals of 260 tons of granite blocks from Penryn to Lambeth for the new bridge. The freight rate for this was 8/- (40p) per ton making a total of £105-1s-0d (£105.5p) including a gratuity of one guinea. While the earnings were nothing special, the voyage to the London river did afford the company chartering office the opportunity of fixing cargoes to the west from London both before and after the stone with the minimum of ballast passages.

In 1934, towards the end of her service with Everard, *Capable* was engaged on a pattern of voyages that the company was to maintain for another 30 years. Coal would be loaded at Keadby and taken at 5/6d (27.5p) per ton to Norwich for the power station. She would then drop down the river to Cantley to load sugar at the sugar beet factory. This was generally consigned to London and carried at 5/3d (26.25p) per ton. Earnings were not spectacular and a fortnight's work produced £133-19-1d. Unfortunately there were few cargoes offering northwards from London and the trip would usually be made in ballast. Ironically three voyages with coal from Keadby to Norwich without any other freights over a similar period produced £204-5-3d (£204.2625p).

In December 1935 *Capable* was sold to John Dennis Sullivan, an owner/master from Westcliff-on-Sea. A later photograph of the ship shows her unchanged since her Everard

Capable anchored in the River Trent. In this later view note the enclosed wheelhouse. *[E. Turner, Author's collection.*

days with the exception of the funnel mark. Unfortunately it is not possible to discern the colours but it looks as though the mark has merely been rotated through 90 degrees so that the red sectors of the original now form a diamond.

The vessel's demise occurred early during the war. When on a voyage from Alderney to Portsmouth with stone she detonated a magnetic mine and sank 2.8 miles from Horsesand Fort at Spithead on 5th June 1940. There were no survivors. In a poignant reminder of the tragedies of war, the event was reported to the London Registrar by the master's wife and executrix and the register was closed on 22nd July 1940.

GRANA/CAPABLE

Auxiliary schooner/motor barge (registered 177/1920 in London)
ON 144446
213.95g 158.25 n
108.6 x 23.1 x 10.0 feet.
2-cyl. Kromhout hot bulb engine by D. Goedkoop, Amsterdam, Netherlands.
2.1918: Completed by Gebroeder Zwolsman, Ulst, Netherlands for N.V. Scheepvaart Maatschappij Grana, Rotterdam, Netherlands (O.C. Sætrang & Co., Skien, Norway, managers) as GRANA.
1919: Sold to O.C. Sætrang (A/S Grana, G.M. Grønvold, manager) Skien but registered in Rotterdam.
4.1919: Sold to A/S Mercur (C.B.

Nielsen, manager) Skien, and registered in Skien.

7.8.1919: Driven ashore in bad weather at Bjönnabben, Sweden while on a ballast passage from Nakskov to Haget, Öland. Abandoned to underwriters.

22.3.1920: Acquired by Frederick Thomas Everard, London; engine repaired or replaced by a similar unit made under license by Plenty and Son Ltd., Newbury.

7.9.1922: Owner became F.T. Everard and Sons Ltd., Greenhithe.

14.4.1925: Cut down to a motor coaster, re-engined with a 4-cyl. 2SA 4P50-type oil engine by Plenty and Son Ltd., Newbury (Works No. 524) and renamed CAPABLE. Tonnages became 216.14g. 128.12n.

13.12.1935: Sold to John Dennis Sullivan, Westcliff-on-Sea, Essex.

5.6.1940: Detonated a mine and sank 2.8 miles from Horsesand Fort at Spithead while on passage from Alderney to Portsmouth with a cargo of stone. There were no survivors.

22.7.1940: Register closed.

Capable now owned by Captain John Sullivan: note the altered funnel mark.
[Nautical Photo Agency/ Author's collection]

BRITISH INDIA'S *ARONDA*

The correspondence concerning P&O and British India in 'Record' 47 inspired Tony Smythe to send this evocative photograph of the latter company's *Aronda*. She was designed for the premier run of the British India Steam Navigation Co. Ltd., the express service from Calcutta to Rangoon, the mail contract calling for an average speed of 16 knots port-to-port including reduced speed in the rivers at each end. The photograph, probably taken in the 1920s, shows her in Calcutta surrounded by local craft and epitomises BI at its peak, when the fleet had reached a total of 161 ships. *Aronda* was requisitioned in August 1914 as an Indian Expeditionary Force transport running between

India and the Mediterranean. Released in 1919, she gave reliable service for the next twenty years. She was sold in March 1939 and was broken up in Bombay. Further details are:

4,062g 1,677n

390.3 x 50.0 x 21.3 feet

Two Q.4-cyl. by Alexander Stephen and Sons Ltd., Govan; 8,800 IHP, 17.64 knots (trials), driving twin screws.

Accommodation for 50 first class, 47 second class and 1,250 deck passengers.

Launched 7.3.1912 and delivered 7.5.1912 by Alexander Stephen and Sons Ltd., Govan (Yard number 449).

THE HOBART SHIP PHOTOGRAPHERS
Russell Priest

The article published in 'Record' 39 entitled 'Overseas Fruit Ships in Hobart 1960-1976', brought to mind the abundance of ship photographers in that Tasmanian port in the three decades after the Second Word War, including the author of the article himself, Rex Cox.

Hobart could only be described as a small port but for some reason it produced in the 1950s a group of keen ship photographers out of proportion to its size and population. It was not uncommon for eight photographers to be lined up at one vantage point to capture a ship moving, especially if it was a first-time caller on a weekend and the conditions were right.

Not only were these photographers, without exception, taking very good material, but some of them were at the forefront of photographic technology, especially the taking of colour transparencies, a medium still in its infancy at a time where large and medium format black and white photography was very much the norm.

The first to use Kodachrome colour transparency film was David Kirby in 1952 and he was followed over the next few years by Lindsay Rex, Roger Martin, Rex Cox, Kingsley Barr and Reg Wilson. They were all known to each other through their membership of the Hobart Branch of the World Ship Society but, unbeknown to them, another photographer, David Cooper, was also taking colour slides of Hobart shipping at the time. His work only came to light in recent times and none of it has ever been published.

Hobart was founded in 1804 at the mouth of the Derwent River and was Australia's second city after Sydney. Famous for its Georgian architecture, it is the southernmost and smallest of the six state capitals with a history inextricably linked to its port, one of the world's finest deep water facilities.

Initially a whaling port, Hobart became a centre for wooden ship building and grew to become a thriving commercial port with its heyday in the mid-twentieth century. It exported fruit, timber, newsprint, zinc, hops and imported general, zinc concentrate, paper pulp and phosphate, but by far the largest export was apples and pears to Great Britain and Europe. This trade was lost when Britain joined the European Economic Community but, prior to then, anything up to 30 ships would call at Hobart to load fruit, mainly apples, during the season.

The availability of cheap hydro-electric power saw the establishment in 1917 of the Electrolytic Zinc Works upriver at Risdon and this brought a further trade in zinc concentrate in and zinc ingots out. A phosphate works at Risdon also required the bulk import of phosphate up the Derwent and under the lift span of the floating bridge which had been opened in 1943 to link Hobart with its rapidly growing eastern shore.

The bridge provided an excellent vantage point for photographers taking the ships going to and from Risdon under the lift span and this continued when the new Tasman Bridge opened in early 1964. The new bridge had a central span high enough above the Derwent to allow navigation and it provided access for pedestrian traffic, which of course included the port's band of intrepid photographers who now took their lives in their hands as they ducked and weaved their way across five lanes of passing traffic to get their stern shots.

The situation remains the same today but was interrupted for three years while the bridge was rebuilt following the collapse of three spans with a tragic loss of life when the Australian National Line bulk carrier *Lake Illawarra* lost steerage way while approaching the central navigation span and drifted into the bridge supports on the eastern side. The ship, full of zinc concentrate, sank immediately and four cars went off the edge into the void. The date was 5th January 1975 and luckily it was 9:27pm on a Sunday night which ensured that traffic on the bridge was comparatively light. The unfortunate *Lake Illawarra*, along with its cargo, remains on the bottom of the river to this day. Her legacy is that traffic is now stopped whenever a largish vessel passes under the bridge, making life much safer of course for the photographers.

The Tasman Bridge and its forerunner, the Hobart Bridge, were by no means the only photographic vantage points in Hobart and in any event only a small percentage of visiting ships ventured up to Risdon. Some of the vessels in Hobart to load apples would first go to Risdon to load zinc ingots for ballast but nowhere near all of them. In those days, when young men on wharves with cameras were not mistaken for terrorists and a family Sunday afternoon outing was often a walk around the wharves looking at the 'boats', it was easy to get good shots from the end of the wharves of vessels arriving and departing. An added advantage in Hobart was the layout of the port itself which allowed for very good alongside shots of ships at many berths.

Not too distant to the south of Hobart lies Port Huon, a one-wharf port where the occasional fruit ship would call for apples and this also provided opportunities for ship photography.

Coastal shipping provided many regular visitors. Tasmania, being the island state, had no interstate road or rail transport; it all came and went by sea. The local company, Holyman, plus Howard Smith, Huddart Parker, Melbourne Steam, Adelaide Steam, Australian National Line and Broken Hill Proprietary, all traded to Hobart and Risdon. The Union Steam Ship Company of New Zealand Ltd. almost had a monopoly on the Tasmanian trade with their Australian-flag tonnage, whilst their New Zealand flag vessels were common callers on the trans-Tasman trade, which indeed was a Union Company monopoly.

The fruit export trade, although dominated by the Conference Lines' British-flag vessels, was not exclusively served by them. Wilhelmsen, Danish East Asiatic, Swedish Transatlantic Rederi, and Royal Interocean Line were among companies commonly seen and later Salen reefers plus an occasional John Lauritzen reefer could also be seen. Neither were fruit ships alone in the overseas trades, as during the cruise season the likes of P&O and Orient Line sent their liners.

Hobart's petroleum products are delivered by product tankers which also pass under the Tasman Bridge on their way to the tank farm at Risdon.

The port had always been a popular call for warships and this remains the case with the deep water and safe anchorage attracting US Navy carriers for rest and recreation; usually it is their last port on the way home at the end of a tour of duty in the Middle East.

Those intrepid ship photographers risking their lives on the Tasman Bridge were the successors of John Craike and Noel Browne who had been photographing Hobart shipping since before the Second World War. When photography was banned during the war, John and Noel were given permits to continue but lost them when they were caught photographing from a boat off Risdon, a restricted area. With their hobby gone for the duration, they both joined up, John in the Armoured Corps and Noel in the Royal Air Force. They resumed their photography after the war and were to be an influence on the new generation of Hobart ship photographers who took up the hobby as young boys in the years immediately following the war.

There was, not unexpectedly, an overlap when they were taking both black and white and colour and this gave rise to considerable angst at times as cameras with their fixed lens were juggled while the subject, underway to Risdon, approached the bridge at a rate of knots.

John and Noel stopped taking photographs in the early 1970s, no doubt unimpressed by containerisation, but Noel, who had also moved into colour, returned to the hobby in 1983. He died in 1989. John lived until 2007. Their early pre-war black and white material seems to have disappeared. Some of John's are with the Maritime Museum of Tasmania but the fate of Noel's is not known.

Kingsley Barr was the most determined of the 1950s group and his enthusiasm did not wane even in the face of containerisation, the end of the Conference Lines, and the eventual demise of Australian-flag coastal shipping, all of which saw the Hobart shipping scene reduced to almost nothing compared to what Kingsley and his compatriots had known in their youth.

Kingsley did not take to colour until the mid 1960s but he then persisted with it right up to his untimely death from cancer in 1997. Like John Craike before him, Kingsley worked for the Tasmania Hydro-Electric Commission and it was not unusual to see a Commission van parked on the Tasman Bridge while Kingsley got his shot. I am told his aim was to photograph 1,000 ships from the bridge and in his last weeks he would be seen struggling up the bridge, camera bag in hand, attempting to make his target. Ironically, he got 999. His skill with the camera was legendary as were the lengths to which he would go to get his shot even driving overnight to northern ports such as Bell Bay, to be there in the morning to capture a woodchipper coming up the Tamar in the early morning light.

All have long since retired from successful careers. Lindsay Rex left Hobart for Melbourne in the mid-1960s and worked as an chemical engineer, he is still active in maritime matters, especially preservation. He returns to Hobart often and invariably catches up with his old compatriots. Lindsay still takes photographs but his interests have narrowed to the more esoteric vessels and preserved historical vessels.

The pioneer of Hobart ship colour photography, David Kirby, stopped taking photographs in the early 1970s. He had a successful career in the State Treasury where he rose through the ranks to become the Auditor General. For the last 19 years he has lived in retirement in Hobart. David's other love is singing in the choir at St. David's Cathedral which he joined at the age of eight in 1941. On Sunday 15th June 1952, David was, for the first time in his life, faced with a momentous decision, should he sing at church or photograph the Bank Line Liberty *Corabank* which was due to a lay up city berth prior to moving up stream to Risdon to discharge her cargo of phosphate? The prospect of sunshine on a Liberty was just too much and David says the morning is etched in his memory The ship won out that day but, although David no longer photographs, he still sings in the choir.

Reg Wilson was interested in ships from an early age. One of his early memories from the late 1930s is being taken into the city by an aunt on a Saturday morning to see Huddart Parker's coastal passenger ship *Zealandia* sail for Sydney. During the Second World War, while attending the Hobart Technical College, he recalls looking out of a class room overlooking the oil wharf and seeing T2 tankers berthed with 'pruned and cocooned' P38 fighters on their decks.

It was in the mid to late 1950s that Reg met up with the other Hobart ship photographers and he started with an old Kodak Retina 35mm camera shooting Kodachrome as well as black and white film, Later on he experimented with Ferriania Color including processing but was always drawn back to Kodachrome even after trying Ektacrome which could be processed locally. It was not long before he started to look for more professional equipment and moved into a Zeiss Contaflex and later still he moved up again to an interchangeable lens Exacta with both wide-angle and telephoto lens including a 240mm which was an immense piece of equipment in those days.

Reg was moved to Sydney by his employer in 1966 but continued his hobby for a good few years there until, like most of us who experienced that era, the interest went out of it following the immense changes occasioned by containerisation.

David Cooper, the boy none of the others knew, was born in Hobart in 1931 and he says his interest in ships just grew. His parents, grandparents and uncles travelled a lot, by ship of course, and sent him postcards of the ships they were on. A startling boyhood memory during the Second World War was unexpectedly seeing a great grey ship escorted by small warships coming into view up the Derwent, it was *Queen Mary* on one of her visits down under to pick up troops. In 1946 David purchased a Box Brownie camera, and once he started working, he moved onto a Kodak folding camera and 620 black and white film. He worked in Britain for 18 months in 1953 and 1954 and it was there that he purchased a 35mm Paxette camera and started using colour slide film. He retired to Wynyard in Northern Tasmania in 1987.

Of all the boys taking photographs in Hobart in the 1950s, only one, Roger Martin, pursued a career at sea. Roger joined Broken Hill Proprietary Ltd. (BHP) as a deck cadet and rose through the ranks to master. His sea-going

A panoramic view of the busy port of Hobart on 14th March 1966 during loading of the annual apple crop. Ships pictured from left to right are *Thala Dan* (barely visible), *Hornby Grange, Port Albany, Duquesa, Port St Lawrence, Belnippon, Empress of Australia* and *Karepo*. Visits from Houlder Brothers vessels were rare, so having two in Hobart together was no doubt sufficient incentive for Noel Brown taking this fine photo.

A contemporary view of Hobart, taken from a light aircraft by Kevin Hussey. Looking north up the Derwent River, it shows the original port area in Sullivans Cove to the left, with most of the old finger piers now gone. The 1970s cargo berths at Macquarie Point are in centre frame, while the Tasman Bridge is at right (on approximately the same site as the former floating bridge), with Selfs Point oil berth and Risdon zinc works beyond.

career afforded him the opportunity to take quality colour shots in most Australian ports and his collection provides a legacy of ships long gone, owned by companies also long gone. Roger also lives in retirement in Hobart.

One of the babies of the group, Rex Cox, started taking black and white photographs with a Box Brownie at age 13 in 1960, but says he did not get serious until

he bought his first single lens reflex camera in 1967. He switched to colour slides in 1971 and took them for 20 years until moving to colour prints in the early 1990s. Rex is retired in Hobart and can still be seen around the port, camera in hand, when the occasion demands.

This band of brothers was gate crashed in 1966 by a female, former physical education teacher, Nancy Jacobs, who had moved into a home on Battery Point overlooking the port approaches. She took most of her shots from there but was also seen at other spots including the Tasman Bridge. Nancy took colour slides until converting to colour prints in the 1990s. She was still taking photographs until she moved to a nursing home in 2006. She died in 2008, just short of her 100th birthday.

Today Hobart is home to the Australian Antarctic Division with the Antarctic Research vessel *Aurora Australis*, the French Antarctic Vessel *L'Astolabe* and the Southern Ocean patrol vessel *Oceanic Viking* stationed there. Antarctic support vessels from the US, China and Russia call during the season. Cruise ships call regularly during the summer and ships still go up to Risdon but these days they are almost exclusively the ubiquitous handy-size bulkers, flagged in places often hard to find on a map.

The band of brothers have aged and the face of shipping has changed almost beyond recognition, but their efforts have left a record of how it used to be.

Through the good graces of Rex Cox, Lindsay Rex, Roger Martin, David Cooper and David Kirby, I was granted access to their collections and that of Kingsley Barr whose collection is in the care of Rex Cox, both colour and black and white, to scan and preserve in electronic format and to make available. Such images as these should not lie unseen in the bottoms of drawers never to be published. We must also be grateful that they had the foresight to use Kodachrome, which has stood the test of time so well. It is perhaps ironic that this article was written at the very time Kodak announced they have ceased manufacturing it.

British Explorer photographed by Roger Martin as she sailed on 4th November 1957 after discharging petroleum products (above). British India's *Carpentaria* was taken from the floating bridge by Reg Wilson on 22nd February 1959 (below).

Kingsley Barr captured Eastern and Australian's *Cathay* dressed for her first Hobart visit, sailing in the late afternoon of 17th September 1974 (top).

Clan Line's *Clan Macdonald*, taken by Lindsay Rex while loading fruit on 17th April 1962 (middle).

This ship prevented David Kirby from attending his church choir. He just had to photograph Andrew Weir's Liberty *Corabank* when she arrived at a lay-by Hobart berth on Sunday morning 15th June 1952, prior to discharging her phosphate cargo at Risdon (bottom).

Loaded down to her marks, Shell's *Daronia* was taken by Roger Martin as she berthed on 10th November 1957 (top).

David Kirby was there when Shaw, Savill and Albion's *Delphic* sailed on 13th March 1954 (middle).

Lindsay Rex's wonderful overhead view of Federal's *Dorset*, taken from the Tasman Bridge en route to Risdon on 28th September 1967 (bottom).

Broken Hill Proprietary's *Iron Kerry* was also taken from the Tasman Bridge by Kingsley Barr on 4th October 1982 (top). A nostalgic example of older BHP tonnage is this view of the coal-fired *Iron Monarch*, taken by Roger Martin in Newcastle, New South Wales on 1st February 1959 (middle). By this time Roger had joined BHP as a deck cadet and his photographic activities were no longer confined to Hobart.

A very good view of a counter stern is afforded by this photo of Union Steam Ship Co's *Kakapo*, taken by Lindsay Rex steaming away from Risdon on 28th December 1957 (bottom).

When Roger Martin took this view of the Australian National Line's *Lake Illawarra* at Whyalla, South Australia in the late 1950s, he was not to know that she would finish her days lying at the base of the Tasman Bridge in his home town of Hobart (top).

Rex Cox caught Austasia's purposeful looking passenger/cargo ship *Malaysia* berthing in Hobart on the 6th April 1972 (middle). She had been Booth's *Hubert* and was transferred within the Vestey Group and renamed in 1964.

After a stay of three weeks, Blue Star Line's *Melbourne Star* looked immaculate as she manoeuvred off the Hobart wharves and was captured by David Kirby on 11th May 1952 (bottom).

Australian National Line's coaster *North Esk* arriving at Hobart on 16th November 1967, by when she had been converted into a self-discharging bulk wheat carrier (top). Taken by Lindsay Rex.
'Keep 'em tall and blue' - Blue Funnel's *Orestes* provided a good example of this when seen by Reg Wilson loading in Hobart for south east Asian ports on 22nd August 1962 (middle).
Orient Line's *Orsova*, still in her original corn-coloured livery, was sailing into Hobart on a cruise when Lindsay Rex took this shot on the morning of 4th February 1961 (bottom).

Union Steam Ship Company's classic coaster *Poolta* is shown underway to Risdon at speed (above). She was photographed by Lindsay Rex on 14th November 1961.

David Cooper ventured to the northern Tasmanian port of Burnie in September 1962 to capture Blue Funnel's *Rhexenor* in beautiful light as she manoeuvred off the wharf (below).

Port Line's beautiful *Port Nelson* returning from Risdon on 6th April 1963 (above). David Kirby was lucky to have a ray of sunshine break through the storm clouds to light her up as he captured the moment.

Designed for Houlder's South American frozen meat trade, *Rippingham Grange* was another rare visitor to the Antipodes. She was in Hobart loading apples when David Kirby took this shot on 15th March 1952 (below).

Lindsay Rex took this overhead view from the old Hobart Bridge as the New Zealand Shipping Company's cadet ship *Rakaia* passed underneath on her way to Risdon on 5th October 1961 (above).

Port Huon, just south of Hobart, was a loading port for apples during the season. Lauritzen's Danish-flag reefer *Roman Reefer* was photographed by Kingsley Barr in June 1982 (top left). Blue Star's war-built standard (and former escort carrier) *South Africa Star*, taken by David Cooper alongside at Hobart on 7th December 1958 (left). Reg Wilson braved the wind on the floating bridge to catch Andrew Weir's *Trentbank* as she returned from Risdon in choppy conditions on 17th November 1962 (below).

Whilst Lauritzen's reefer tonnage may have been only occasional visitors to Hobart, the company's small ice-strengthened general cargo vessels were chartered by the Australian government for their Antarctic programme and subsequently became closely associated with the port. Kingsley Barr photographed their *Thala Dan* on 5th December 1981 (above).

To find a colour view of a very old ship is rare, but David Cooper took a slide of Union Steam Ship Company's 1930-built *Waimarino* at Hobart on 8th May 1956 (below). Seldom seen outside of New Zealand waters, she was sold the following year.

THE CLIPPER FAMILY OF REEFER VESSELS
Part 2
Tony Breach

Fleet list entries are in the usual Ships in Focus style. Unless stated otherwise, the flag of the vessel is that of the owning company, the first name in the ownership entry. Names of beneficial owners, where known, are given in brackets before those of the managers.

Built by Smith's Dock Co. Ltd., South Bank, Middlesbrough

Yard No. 1318 **EDINBURGH CLIPPER**
O.N. 357471 IMO 7203364
6,680/4,938g 9,913/2,636n 7,722d
140.75 (131.48) x 18.04 x 11.64 metres
Refrigerated capacity: 352,294 cubic feet.
Sulzer 9RND68 oil engine 9-cyl. 2SCSA by George Clark and North Eastern Marine Engineering Co. Ltd., Wallsend-on-Tyne; 14,850 BHP, 23 knots.
19.1.1972: Launched for Chichester Shipping Lines Ltd., North West Shipping Co. Ltd. and Island Fruit Shipping Co.

Ltd., London (Maritime Fruit Carriers Co. Ltd., Haifa, Israel) as EDINBURGH CLIPPER.
1976: Sold to the Cunard Steam-ship Co. Ltd. (Cunard-Brocklebank Ltd., managers), London and renamed ALSATIA.
1981: Sold to Alaska Maritime Co. S.A., Panama (Enterprises Shipping and Trading S.A. (S. Restis), Piraeus, Greece) and renamed AMERICA FREEZER under the Greek flag.
1985: Sold to Daiko Shipping Ltd., Monrovia, Liberia (Enterprises Shipping and Trading S.A. (S. Restis), Piraeus, Greece) and renamed ANGELMAR under the Greek flag.
1990: Sold to Nema Compania Naviera S.A., Panama (Transcontinental Maritime and Trading S.A., Piraeus, Greece) and renamed ATLANTICO under the Bahamas flag.
1990: Sold to Lucida Navigation S.A.,

Panama (Transcontinental Maritime and Trading S.A., Piraeus, Greece) and renamed NETWORK SWAN under the Bahamas flag.
1991: Sold to Del-Monte Fresh Fruit (International) Ltd., Monrovia, Liberia (Irgens Larsen A/S, Oslo, Norway, managers).
1992: Owners became Del-Monte Fresh Fruit (International) Ltd., Panama City, Panama (Network Shipping Ltd., Coral Gables, Florida) (Irgens Larsen A/S, Oslo, Norway, managers).
1992: Ultimate owners became Del-Monte Fresh Fruit International Ltd., Hamilton, Bermuda and renamed BANANA REEFER.
2.9.1994: Arrived in Chittagong Roads following sale to breakers.
23.9.1994: Demolition began by Diamond Steel Products Co. (Private) Ltd. at Bhatiary, Bangladesh.

Alsatia, the former *Edinbughh Clipper*. *[FotoFlite incorpoarating Skyfotos 244775]*

London Clipper in Salen funnel colours. *[FotoFlite/David Whiteside collection]*

Yard No. 1319 **LONDON CLIPPER**
ON 357483 IMO 7214571
6,680/4,938g 3,638/2,636n 9,193/7,722d
140.70 (131.48) x 18.00 x 11.64 metres
Refrigerated capacity: 352,294 cubic feet.
Sulzer 9RND68 2SCSA oil engine by
George Clark and North Eastern Marine
Engineering Co. Ltd., Wallsend-on-Tyne;
14,850 BHP, 23.0 knots.
12.5.1972: Launched for Javel Ltd., Island Fruit
Reefers Co. Ltd., and North West Shipping Co.
Ltd., London (Maritime Fruit Carriers Co. Ltd.,
Haifa) as LONDON CLIPPER.
8.1972: Completed.

22.10.1976: Sold to Kaplana Shipping Co.
Ltd., Glasgow (W. Bruns Co., Hamburg)
(North Shipping and Forwarding, Preston)
and renamed SALINAS.
9.1978: Transferred to Intercontinental
Transportation Services Ltd., Monrovia
(Standard Fruit and Steamship Co., New
Orleans, USA) (Irgens Larsen A/S, Oslo,
managers) and renamed TROPICAL
BREEZE.
1984: Owners became Mahele Reefer Ltd.,
Monrovia. (Standard Fruit and Steamship
Co., New Orleans, USA).
1986: Transferred to Compania Naviera

Agmaresa S.A., Guayaquil, Ecuador
(Standard Fruit and Steamship Co., New
Orleans, USA) (Irgens Larsen A/S, Oslo,
managers) and renamed RIO SANTA
ROSA.
1992: Beneficial owners became Dole Fresh
Fruit International Ltd., San Jose, Costa
Rica.
1993: Registered in Liberia.
2.10.1993: Arrived Chittagong for
demolition.
17.10.1993: Demolition commenced by
Evergreen Shipbreaking Industries, Sitalpur.

London Clipper as *Rio Santa Rosa*. *[David Whiteside collection]*

Glasgow Clipper (above) and as *Balmar* (below right).   *[Both: FotoFlite incorporating Skyfotos/David Whiteside collection]*

Yard No. 1320 **GLASGOW CLIPPER**
O.N. 357490 IMO 7224629
6,680/4,938g 3,638/2,636n 9,144/7,742d
140.75 (131.48) x 18.04 x 9.04 metres
Refrigerated capacity: 352,294 cubic feet.
Sulzer 9RND68 2SCSA oil engine by
George Clark and North Eastern Marine
Engineering Co. Ltd., Wallsend-on-Tyne;
14,850 BHP, 23 knots.
11.7.1972: Launched for Sovertur Shipping
Co. Ltd., North West Shipping Co. Ltd.
and Island Fruit Shipping Co. Ltd., London
(Maritime Fruit Carriers Co. Ltd., Haifa,
Israel) as GLASGOW CLIPPER.
1976: Sold to the Cunard Steam-ship Co.
Ltd. (Cunard-Brocklebank Ltd., managers),
London and renamed ANDANIA
1981: Sold to Acadimos Maritime Co.
S.A. Panama (Enterprises Shipping and
Trading S.A. (S. Restis), Piraeus, Greece)
and renamed EUROPA FREEZER under the
Greek flag.
1986: Sold to Ribarosa Shipping Ltd.,
Monrovia, Liberia (Enterprises Shipping and
Trading S.A. (S. Restis), Piraeus, Greece) and
renamed BALMAR under the Greek flag.
1990: Sold to Ultima Compania Naviera
S.A., Panama (Transcontinental Maritime
and Trading S.A., Piraeus, Greece) and
renamed PACIFICO under the Bahamas flag.
1990: Sold to Oriental Galaxy S.A.,
Panama (Transcontinental Maritime and
Trading S.A., Piraeus, Greece) and renamed
NETWORK STORK under the Bahamas
flag.
1991: Sold to Del-Monte Fresh Fruit
(International) Ltd., Monrovia, Liberia
(Irgens Larsen A/S, Oslo, Norway,
managers).

1992: Owners became Del-Monte Fresh
Fruit (International) Ltd. Panama City,
Panama (Network Shipping Ltd., Coral
Gables, Florida, USA) (Irgens Larsen A/S,
Oslo, managers).
1992: Ultimate owners became Del-
Monte Fresh Fruit International Ltd.,
Hamilton, Bermuda and renamed BANANA
PLANTER under the Panama flag.
14.1.1995: Laid up at Malalag Bay.
29.4.1995: Beached at Alang.
14.5.1995: Demolition began by Virat
Shipbreaking Corporation.

Yard No. 1321 **TEESSIDE CLIPPER**
O.N. 357505 IMO 7233735
6,680/4,938g 3,638/2,636n 9,145/7,689d
140.75 (131.48) x 18.06 x 11.64 metres
Refrigerated capacity: 352,294 cubic feet.

Sulzer 9RND68 2SCSA oil engine by
George Clark and North Eastern Marine
Engineering Co. Ltd., Wallsend-on-Tyne;
14,850 BHP, 23 knots
20.11.1972: Launched for Curtis Shipping
Co. Ltd. and others, London (Maritime
Fruit Carriers Co. Ltd., Haifa, Israel) as
TEESSIDE CLIPPER.
1976: Sold to the Cunard Steam-ship Co.
Ltd. (Cunard-Brocklebank Ltd., managers),
London and renamed ANDRIA
1981: Sold to Akropol Navigation Co. S.A.,
Panama (Enterprises Shipping and Trading
S.A. (S. Restis), Piraeus, Greece) and
renamed AUSTRALIA FREEZER under the
Greek flag.
1986: Sold to Rubisun Marine S.A.,
Monrovia, Liberia (Enterprises Shipping and
Trading S.A. (S. Restis), Piraeus, Greece)

and renamed CHILLY under the Greek flag.

1987: Sold to Acechilly Navigation Co. Ltd., Valletta, Malta (Government of Cuba, Havana) and renamed ACECHILLY.

1988: Sold to Durango Shipping Co. Ltd., Limassol, Cyprus (Laskaridis Shipping Co. Ltd., Piraeus, Greece) and renamed FRIO HAMBURG.

1993: Sold to Marine Shield S.A., Panama (Laskaridis Shipping Co. Ltd., Piraeus, Greece).

1994: Sold to UB Shipping Ltd. (Ugland Interocean Management Ltd.), London and renamed BANANOR under the Panama flag.

1996: Sold to Ugland Reefers Ltd. (Ugland International Holdings plc), Grand Cayman, Cayman Islands.

1998: Renamed UB PRUDENT.

12.1998: Sold to Green Navigation Ltd. (Star Entech Ltd.), St. Vincent and renamed PRIDE III.

17.1.1999: Arrived at Mumbai to be broken up.

Teesside Clipper (top) in Salen colours and as briefly renamed *UB Prudent* in 1998 (right). *[FotoFlite incorporating Skyfotos/David Whiteside collection; FotoFlite incorporating Skyfotos 221950]*

Yard No.1322 **NEWCASTLE CLIPPER**
ON 357501 IMO 7233747
6,680/4,938g 3,638/2,636n 9,114/7,646d
140.70 (131.25) x 18.00 x 11.64 metres
Refrigerated capacity: 352,294 cubic feet.
Sulzer 9RND68 2SCSA oil engine by
George Clark and North Eastern Marine
Engineering Co. Ltd., Wallsend; 14,850
BHP, 23 knots.
20.11.1972: Launched for Rockhampton
Shipping Co. Ltd. (North West Shipping Co.
Ltd.), Glasgow (Maritime Fruit Carriers Co.
Ltd., Haifa) as NEWCASTLE CLIPPER.
3.1973: Completed for Sovertur Shipping
Co. Ltd. and others (North West Shipping
Co. Ltd.), Glasgow.
1976: Sold to Blue Star Line Ltd. (Blue
Star Ship Management Ltd.), London and
renamed TROJAN STAR.
1980: Sold to Saful Navigation Inc. (S.
Palios) (Diana Shipping Agencies S.A.),
Piraeus, Greece and renamed CHIOS
CLIPPER.
5.2.1991: Accommodation seriously
damaged by fire while loading bananas at
Puerto Limon, Costa Rica and laid up at that
port. The claim by the Dole organisation
for the loss of cargo, ballast bonus and hire
differential during this incident amounted to
$1,811,477 but this was never recovered.
1992: Sold in damaged condition to Blue
Navigation Corporation, Piraeus and
renamed FRIO CLIPPER.
21.8.1992: Left Puerto Limon for Piraeus
where she arrived for repairs on 22.10.1992.
1994: Sold to Roman Hurricane Shipping
Ltd. (Sumo Shipmanagement Ltd.),
Kingstown, St. Vincent and renamed
ROMAN HURRICANE.

Newcastle Clipper as *Trojan Star* (above) and as *Roman Hurricane* arriving at Aliaga for demolition in April 1995. *[David Whiteside collection; Selim San]*

Alaunia. [FotoFlite incorporating Skyfotos 270440]

30.10.1994: Arrived Midia for repairs to damage incurred during February 1991 but was found to be not worth repairing.
12.4.1995: Arrived at Aliaga for demolition.
19.6.1995: Work commenced by Nigtas Gemi Sokum Ticaret A.S.

Yard No. 1323 **CARDIFF CLIPPER**
O.N. 361584 IMO 7306192
6,690/4,938g 3,638/2,636n 9,145/7,689d
140.75 (131.48) x 18.04 x 11.64 metres
Refrigerated capacity: 352,294 cubic feet.
Sulzer 9RND68 2SCSA oil engine by George Clark and North Eastern Marine Engineering Co. Ltd., Wallsend-on-Tyne; 14,850 BHP, 23 knots.
6.3.1973: Launched by Smith's Dock Co. Ltd., South Bank, Middlesbrough as CARDIFF CLIPPER.
6.1973: Completed for Cardigan Bay Shipping Co. Ltd., London (Maritime Fruit Carriers Co. Ltd., Haifa, Israel).
1974: Owners became Abeyreuth Shipping Co. Ltd. and Adelaide Shipping Lines Ltd., London (Maritime Fruit Carriers Co. Ltd., Haifa, Israel).
1976: Sold to the Cunard Steam-ship Co. Ltd. (Cunard-Brocklebank Ltd., managers), London and renamed ALAUNIA.
1981: Sold to Amorgos Maritime Co. S.A., Panama (S. Restis) (Enterprises Shipping and Trading S.A., Piraeus, Greece) and renamed OCEANIA FREEZER under the Greek flag.
1986: Sold to Laval Maritime Ltd., Monrovia, Liberia (S. Restis) (Enterprises Shipping and Trading S.A., Piraeus, Greece) and renamed FROSTY under the Greek flag.
1987: Sold to Acefrosty Navigation Co. Ltd., Valletta, Malta (Government of Cuba, Havana) and renamed ACEFROSTY.
1988: Sold to Mazatlan Shipping Co. Ltd., Limassol, Cyprus (Laskaridis Shipping Co. Ltd., Piraeus, Greece) and renamed FRIO BREMEN.
1993: Owners became Lilium Maritime

S.A., Panama (Laskaridis Shipping Co. Ltd., Piraeus, Greece).
1994: Sold to UB Shipping Ltd. (Ugland Interocean Management Ltd.), London and renamed GOLDEN B under the Panama flag.

1996: Sold to Ugland Reefers Ltd. (Ugland International Holdings plc), Grand Cayman, Cayman Islands.
1997: Renamed UB PEARL.
2.11.1998: Arrived Alang to be broken up having been sold to Global Investors Ltd.

Cardiff Clipper under three names: *Acefrosty* (top), a heavily smoking *Frio Bremen* (middle) and *UB Pearl* (bottom). *[FotoFlite incorporating Skyfotos 270955; David Whiteside collection; FotoFlite incorporating Skyfotos 223334]*

Yard No. 1324 **BRISTOL CLIPPER**
ON 351594 IMO 7324089
6,680/4,938g 3,638/2,636n 9,144/7,689d
140.70 (130.00) x 18.01 x 11.64 metres
Refrigerated capacity: 352,294 cubic feet.
Sulzer 9RND68 2SCSA oil engine by
George Clark and North Eastern Marine
Engineering Co. Ltd., Wallsend-on-Tyne;
14,850 BHP, 23.0 knots.
1.7.1973: Launched for Bristol Maritime
Enterprises Co. Ltd., London (Maritime
Fruit Carriers Co. Ltd., Haifa) as
BRISTOL CLIPPER.
11.1973: Completed for Farmcol Ltd.,
Island Fruit Reefers Shipping Co. Ltd.,
and North West Shipping Co. Ltd., London
(Maritime Fruit Carriers Co. Ltd., Haifa).
1976: Transferred to Marshtrim Ltd.,
London and renamed KING EDMUND.
1977: Sold to VEB Deutfracht/Seerederei
(DSR Reefers), Rostock, East Germany
and renamed ERNST MORITZ ARNDT.
13. 9.1990: Sold to Elmshurst Shipping
Ltd., Douglas, Isle of Man (Cool Ship
Management, Stockholm, Sweden) and
renamed BAGNO CATARAMA under the
Panama flag.
27.4.1994: Arrived at Alang for demolition.
14.5.1994: Work commenced by Vikas
Shipping Corporation.

Bristol Clipper as the East German *Ernst Moritz Arndt* (above) and the Panama-flag *Bagno Catarama* (below). *[FotoFlite incorporating Skyfotos126603 and 334224]*

Yard No. 1325 **LIVERPOOL CLIPPER**
ON 351698 IMO 7329352
6,680/4,938g 3,638/2,636n 9,144/7,689d
140.70 (130.00) x 18.00 x 11.64 metres
Refrigerated capacity: 352,294 cubic feet.
Sulzer 9RND68 2SCSA oil engine by
George Clark and North Eastern Marine
Engineering Co. Ltd., Wallsend-on-Tyne;
14,850 BHP, 23.0 knots.
12.9.1973: Launched for Portland
Bay Shipping Co. Ltd., London as
LIVERPOOL CLIPPER
1.1974: Completed for Coinworth Ltd.,
Island Fruit Reefers Shipping Co. Ltd.,
and North West Shipping Co. Ltd., London
(Maritime Fruit Carriers Co. Ltd., Haifa,
Israel) (Whitco Marine Services Ltd.,
London, managers).
1976: Transferred to Mainquill Ltd.,
London and renamed KING EGBERT.
1978: Sold to VEB Deutfracht/Seerederei
(DSR Reefers), Rostock, East Germany
and renamed GERHART HAUPTMANN.
1990: Sold to Elmshurst Shipping
Ltd., Douglas, Isle of Man (Cool Ship
Management, Stockholm) and renamed
BAGNO QUEVEDO under the Panama
flag.
1992: Renamed BILLE FROST.
29. 1.1994: Arrived at Sydney, Nova
Scotia with hull fractures sustained during
a voyage from Souris to Puerto Cabello
with a cargo of potatoes. Detained
by Canadian Coast Guard and cargo
discharged.
8.4.1994: Sailed Sydney for Alang.
5.5.1994: Arrived Alang.
11.5.1994: Delivered to breakers and
beached.

King Egbert. [FotoFlite incorporating Skyfotos/David Whiteside collection]

Built by Framnaes Mekaniska & Vaerksted A/S, Sandefjord, Norway.

Heinrich Heine as built (top), as *Metonic* (middle) and *Nafplio* (bottom). *[FotoFlite incorporating Skyfotos 340636; David Whiteside collection (2)]*

Yard No.184 **HEINRICH HEINE**
IMO 7383140 6,640g 3,612n 9,146d
140.72 (130.00) x 17.99 x 11.64
metres
Refrigerated capacity: 361,608 cubic feet.
Sulzer 8RND68 2SCSA oil engine by A/S Horten Verft, Horten, Norway; 13,200 BHP, 22.75 knots.
1975: Launched for VEB Deutfracht/ Seerederei (DSR Reefers), Rostock, East Germany as HEINRICH HEINE.
30.6.1975: Completed.
2.4.1988: Badly damaged in a collision in the River Elbe with the Indonesian motor vessel MATARAM (IMO 7920601, 13,445/1981) during a voyage from Rostock to Cuba. Repaired at Cuxhaven and Hamburg.
27.9.1990: Sold to Elmshurst Shipping Ltd., Douglas, Isle of Man (Cool Ship Management, Stockholm, Sweden) and renamed BAGNO EL TRIUNFO under the Panama flag.
1994: Sold to Metonic Compania Naviera S.A., Panama (Teo Shipping Corporation, Piraeus, Greece) (Fairport Shipping Ltd., Piraeus) and renamed METONIC.
1996: Sold to Transmarine Development S.A., Panama (Costas Comninos) (International Reefer Services S.A., Piraeus, Greece) and renamed NAFPLIO.
12. 5.1998: Detained at St. Petersburg for over a year in respect of a claim for cargo damage.
12.2009: Still in existence.

Yard No.185 **THEODOR KORNER**
IMO 7383152 6,641g 3,612n 9,146d
140.70 (130.00) x 18.00 x 11.64
metres
Refrigerated capacity: 361,608 cubic
feet
Sulzer 8RND68 2SCSA oil engine by
A/S Horten Verft, Horten, Norway;
13,200 BHP, 22.75 knots.
30.6.1975: Launched for VEB
Deutfracht/Seerederei, 'DSR
Reefers', Rostock, East Germany as
THEODOR KORNER.
18.12.1975: Completed.
1990: Sold to Elmshurst Shipping
Ltd., Douglas, Isle of Man (Cool
Ship Management, Stockholm,
Sweden) and renamed BAGNO
ESMERALDAS under the Panama flag.
1994: Sold to Magellanic Compania
Naviera S.A., Panama (Teo Shipping
Corporation, Piraeus, Greece)
(Fairport Shipping Ltd., Piraeus) and
renamed MAGELLANIC.
3.1996: Sold to Transmarine Carriers
S.A., Panama (Costas Comninos)
(International Reefer Services S.A.,
Piraeus) and renamed ARGOLIC.
1999: Sold to Anteus Shipping S.A.
(Eurotrust Holdings), Panama and
renamed VISTA I.
2000: Sold to First Star Transport,
Phnom Penh, Cambodia (Ost-West
Handel und Schiffahrt G.m.b.H.,
Bremen, Germany) and renamed
EISHA under the flag of St. Vincent
and the Grenadines.
30.8.2008: Beached at Alang for
demolition.

To be concluded

DSR's *Theodor Korner* (top) is shown also as *Argolic* (middle) and *Eisha* (bottom).
[FotoFlite incorporating Skyfotos 69014; David Whiteside collection (2)]

HALAL UPDATE

K.S. Garrett

Since publication of my article on the Halal Shipping Co. Ltd. in 'Record' 46, it has been a great pleasure to talk and exchange correspondence with Captain H. Roberts who sailed with the company from 1953 to 1957. He has been kind enough to share his experiences with me and naturally he was able to tell me much more about the company and its founder than I had managed to glean from official records or dredge from my own memory. He also sent me copies of articles relating to the company. Further help has been received from David Tranter and R. Clucas.

The founder, Antonin Besse was in fact a Provencal Frenchman although in a couple of lists of his company's directors he is described as Belgian. This is probably explained by the fact that he married a Belgian lady and based himself in Brussels for a number of years. He had originally worked for a French firm in Aden but in 1902 he set up on his own at Hodeidah as a coffee exporter. Goatskins were also exported and the principal imports were sugar, cotton goods and cigarettes. His commercial empire grew and he built an impressive office with warehousing and his own living accommodation in Aden.

As the years passed these activities grew and Besse imported into Aden hides of all kinds from Ethiopia, Eritrea and from French, Italian and British Somaliland. Coffee came from Yemen and Ethiopia, frankincense from Hadramaut and Somaliland and myrrh from Somaliland. All these goods were later exported to Europe. The firm also imported and distributed textiles, machinery, motor cars and tyres, radios, electrical goods, cigarettes, pharmaceuticals and air conditioning units.

In the period just after the First World War the main supplier of the kerosene used for lighting and cooking in the area was the US oil giant, SOCONY and it was brought in large shipments from Port Arthur in Texas. It was imported in cans to Aden and distributed from there by dhows or the small elderly steamships of the Cowasjee Dinshaw company which was a major competitor of Antonin Besse. Because of the large individual shipments many of the cans of kerosene had to remain for long periods in storage. This in itself was expensive but the cans also deteriorated in store.

Besse was visited by a hard-driving marketing manager from Shell and more or less challenged to start shipping Shell products from Suez to Aden. Given a suitable, small ship, individual loads would be more economic and the ship itself could deliver much of the oil to many of the ports in the area without the use of dhows, storage or double handling. This would challenge the virtual monopoly held by SOCONY and also his local rival Cowasjee Dinshaw.

It was a very tempting prospect but Shell made it clear that no financial assistance would be forthcoming. Besse had had some very serious financial problems and at the time was still struggling to survive but he decided to go ahead and raised the necessary capital. He mortgaged the ship to the shipbuilder. The Shell company did help with technical assistance although this was not totally altruistic as it was in their own interest that the project was successful. The first ship, *Halal* of 344 gross tons, entered service in 1924 and sailed to the Middle East to load her first Shell cargo at Suez.

Success seems to have been immediate and Besse soon ordered a second ship but by this time Shell were more amenable to providing financial assistance. She was the *El Amin* and came into service in 1926. She was mortgaged to Shell who also took the mortgage on the earlier *Halal.*

Shortly after coming into service the *El Amin* had the misfortune to go aground on rocks at Ras Mesalle near Suez during a ballast passage from Port Sudan to Suez. Salvage and the subsequent repairs were both expensive and lengthy requiring a dry dock and replacement of almost half of the ship's bottom and tank top plating. She was out of action for two months and this led to a decrease in Shell's recently established local business. The oil company realised how exposed they were to such disruptions and immediately offered a mortgage and technical assistance for Besse to build a third ship. This was the *El Hak* and she entered service in 1929.

Very soon Besse had over seventy percent of the regional trade and this continued to rise. He was able to distribute the oil directly to many of the small anchorage ports thus reducing the reliance on dhows, although some were still used for small transhipments to more restricted places. Besse had his own fleet of dhows, built by his own yard at Ma'alla. Some of the larger ones had diesel engines fitted to enable them to trade into the monsoon. In a very short time Besse was the principal supplier in the region of Shell products, the most important of which in the early days was the kerosene or paraffin used in lamps and Primus stoves that were essential features of life.

In 1928 Shell and the Anglo-Persian Oil company, later British Petroleum, agreed to merge their marketing in the area and formed the Consolidated Petroleum Company to carry out the business. Besse retained the Shell business and also obtained that of British Petroleum This large enterprise was managed from the Besse office in Aden. The Shell products were now shipped from Port Sudan in 'Gazelle' containers and the British

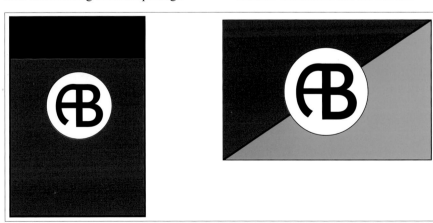

Funnel and flag of the Halal Shipping Co. Ltd.

Petroleum products came from Abadan in 'Palm Tree' containers.

Besse also acted as a ships' agent in Aden and this activity was beneficial to other parts of his empire. Ships always seem to require repair and it was only natural for this work to be directed towards the Besse Marine Workshop. To improve his repair facilities Besse purchased a floating dock from the Admiralty in 1947; this had been sunk in Massawa by the Italians but was subsequently raised and repaired. At first intended for use by the Halal ships to reduce the expense of using docks in Suez or Mombasa, it was also used by outside ships. He had many other local interests being the owner of the Crescent Hotel and the Chairman and a shareholder in Aden Airways.

The Halal ships carried very large crews for their size with 60 or 70 men being quite usual. This should be compared with a similar-sized British coaster in north western Europe where perhaps just ten men were carried. The senior officers were generally British and the juniors very often Indian. On deck the ships carried a complement of ratings very similar in structure to Indian-crewed ships with a serang, burra tindal, chota tindal, cassab, sekunnis and kalassis. Maybe they had a mistri wallah and a topaz or two. It would be very similar in the engine room with a serang, tindals, cassab, drivers and tal wallahs. The catering department was headed by the Butla who had charge of cooks, pantry man and the various stewards or boys and of course the dhobi wallahs. He was also in charge of the crew's cooks or bandaris. Added to this impressive list there was also a separate gang of coolies under the coolie tindal who operated the deck cranes and were generally concerned with the cargo and preparation of the

cargo holds. Imagine all these together with several hundred deck passengers about to make their pilgrimage. It is quite remarkable, although it has to be said that given the paucity of facilities in the region, once they left Aden these ships had to be self sustaining and rely completely on their own resources.

There were also two very important Yemeni clerks known as kuranis. In fact, they were more than just clerks or writers but carried out some of the work normally done by a purser. They also had a hand in some of the cargo documentation. It is thought that they might well have carried out some private enterprise and may have been actively encouraged to do this.

During the 1950s some of the smaller Red Sea ports were dropped from regular schedules and some of the later ships also ventured from the Red Sea to the eastern Mediterranean calling at Alexandria, Limassol, Famagusta, Lattakia and Beirut (known as the Paris of the Middle East) before returning through the Suez canal to the Red Sea. The company's operations also extended southwards down the east African coast to Mogadiscio and Mombassa.

Naturally the ships all had their own peculiarities and some entered into company folklore. The *El Hak* of 1929 so pleased Antonin Besse that he called her 'My little jewel of the Red Sea' when she arrived in Aden on her maiden voyage. With the post-war *El Halal* the builders, Ardrossan Shipyard, obviously made a miscalculation and the ship had a stability problem and a permanent list which had to be rectified by 200 tons of permanent ballast under number 2 hold with the consequent loss of deadweight and earnings. The following ship, *El Kerym*, had no such problem but Antonin Besse managed to obtain a rebate to compensate for the losses

incurred by the earlier ship to reduce the price of the new ship.

The ships had a very basic outfit of navigational equipment and, given the lack of aids to navigation in their area of operations, it is surprising that none of them carried radar. At the time radar sets were rather rudimentary compared with developments only a few years along the line, but at least they would have given a reasonably accurate idea of the distance off an island or the mainland unless of course it was very low-lying. Maybe Besse was one of those ship owners who subscribed to the view that given radar his officers would relax their normal cautious vigilance and adopt a dangerous gung ho attitude!

Antonin Besse died in 1951 while visiting his friend Kurt Hahn at Gordonstoun School. In that same year he had received a KBE from the Colonial Office List while he had been made a member of the French Legion d'Honneur in 1949. He had also been made a Doctor of Civil Law at Oxford University in recognition of his gift of £1.5 million to found and endow St. Antony's College. A remarkable man.

Glossary

Bandari	crew's cook
Burra tindal	senior bosun's mate
Butla	chief steward/ catering manager
Cassab	storekeeper and lamp trimmer
Chota tindal	junior bosun's mate
Dhobi wallah	laundryman
Kalassi	sailor
Kurani	clerk
Mistri wallah	carpenter
Sekunni	quartermaster
Serang	bosun
Tal wallah	greaser
Topaz	sweeper

SOURCES AND ACKNOWLEDGEMENTS

We thank all who gave permission for their photographs to be used, and for help in finding photographs we are particularly grateful to Tony Smith, Jim McFaul and David Whiteside of the World Ship Photo Library; to Ian Farquhar, F.W. Hawks, Peter Newall, William Schell; and to David Hodge and Bob Todd of the National Maritime Museum, and other museums and institutions listed.

Research sources have included the *Registers* of William Schell and Tony Starke, 'Lloyd's Register', 'Lloyd's Confidential Index', 'Lloyd's Shipping Index', 'Lloyd's War Losses', 'Mercantile Navy Lists', 'Marine News', 'Sea Breezes' and 'Shipbuilding and Shipping Record'. Use of the facilities of the World Ship Society,

the Guildhall Library, the National Archives and Lloyd's Register of Shipping and the help of Dr Malcolm Cooper are gratefully acknowledged. Particular thanks also to Bob Todd for proof reading, Heather Fenton for editorial and indexing work, and to Marion Clarkson for accountancy services.

Capable

Thanks to J.D. van der Baan, M. Lindenborn, E.A. Kruidhof, R. Walsh, V. Allen, C. Burnett and E. Wildsmith for their help in the preparation of this article. Registration documents for *Capable* are in the National Archives in files BT110/1199 and CUST130/107.

A PRINCE LINE MYSTERY

John Dobson

There is but little evidence to support the proposed existence of the Prince Line steamers *Piedmontese Prince* and the *Sardinian Prince*, a story which is mentioned from time to time, most recently in 'Record' 41. What there is, however, brings up the question of interpretation of the available evidence. The generally accepted story is that Prince Line had two emigrant steamers building at Sunderland and, because of political events in Italy, sold them on the stocks to the new Italian shipowner Lloyd Sabaudo. The following is an interpretation of what evidence the writer has come across when trying to confirm this story.

Migration is an important aspect of the history and make-up of the United States of America. In the nineteenth and twentieth centuries most of the migrants came across the Atlantic. Prince Line was involved in this process from 1897 until it withdrew in 1908. In 1898, for the first time, there were more immigrants entering the United States from Italy than from any other country. The poverty and overpopulation of Italy was the impetus for these people to try and make a new life or possibly their fortune in the New World, which many did and then returned to their homeland.

In the early 1890s James Knott decided to move from general trading to establishing liner trades. He had traded with Italy mainly carrying coal from the Tyne to Civitavecchia and Genoa since 1882 before establishing a service between Italy and New York. Prince Line entered the Italian emigrant trade with the *Trojan Prince* (1896/3,273), which was transferred from the South American service and left New York on 26th September 1897 for Genoa, Leghorn and Naples. She was joined by the *Tartar Prince* (1895/3,272), another South American ship,

and the new *Spartan Prince* ((1897/3,299) which made her maiden voyage from New York on 16th January 1898 after a positioning trip in ballast from her builder's yard. These three ships provided three-weekly sailings from New York to Italy, sometimes with calls at the Azores. In 1902 the ships were transferred to other services with the acquisition of the *Rei de Portugal* and *Alvares Cabral* which became the emigrant ships *Napolitan Prince* (1889/3,236) and *Sicilian Prince* (1889/2,784). At over 14 knots these two vessels were faster than the ships they were replacing and the trade was operated by the two ships on an approximately four-week sailing frequency from New York.

Early in 1907 the first sign of competition arose when the service was extended to include some Greek ports, but this only lasted about 12 months. In a speech made in 1906 a very confident James Knott stated 'Last year 21 shipping companies, the Prince Line amongst them, carried one million and a quarter emigrants to New York. This year we shall carry a million and a half, and they will hardly touch the fringe of the demand'. His optimism was overtaken by events, in the form of a price war, so his service was terminated and the ships were laid up in Naples in the early part of 1908. This was the end of the emigrant trade for Prince Line.

On 28th December 1908 there was a tremendous earthquake which affected Sicily and southern Italy. The epicentre was near the port of Messina which was partly destroyed. James Knott offered the Italian Government the two laid-up vessels for hospital purposes. The Italians accepted the offer and used the *Sicilian Prince* for accommodation at Naples. The *Napolitan Prince* was

Napolitan Prince. [J. and M. Clarkson collection]

used to ferry earthquake victims from Messina to Genoa. Eventually these ships were brought to the Tyne and laid up for a long period and found new owners only in 1911.

In 1905 the Italian Government sponsored a subsidy scheme for Italian merchant ships. First to benefit from this new legislation were shipbuilders, including those in the United Kingdom. They received several orders, including the Sunderland yard of Sir James Laing and Sons, which built three ships for Lloyd Sabaudo of Genoa. These ships - contracts 621, 622 and 623 - were taken on by Laings at a difficult time for the company. As the history of Wear shipbuilding, 'Where Ships are Born', puts it: 'A few years after Sir James Laing's death, the firm got into financial difficulties. There was a big loss on a contract for three large vessels for the Italian emigrant trade.' This loss accrued because the contract included a two-way clause in which a bonus was to be paid for an increase in speed above 15 knots within a specified fuel consumption, but conversely there was a penalty for not meeting design speed and fuel consumption. The latter proved to be the case.

The first and only time the writer has come across the names *Piedmontese Prince* and *Sardinian Prince* was in a contemporary sense was in the weekly fleet list for Prince Line published in Newcastle newspapers in September 1908.

An interpretation of the story so far would be as follows. Because of the price war in this trade Prince Line withdrew their existing ships and may have been negotiating to charter two ships under the Italian flag thereby gaining the advantages of the Italian Government subsidy. Unfortunately for Prince Line, the Italian Government came under pressure from other Italian industries and the subsidy came to an end about this time. This ruled out a joint Prince Line/Italian venture as the advantage of using Italian subsidised ships with the inherent operating cost saving had been removed. The two names only appeared once in the weekly Prince Line fleet list, but the advertising people were quick off the mark as about this time a Prince Line advertisement appeared featuring a ship very similar to the Lloyd Sabaudo vessels. Hence the supposition that the charter could have involved two of the three steamers.

A parallel interpretation of this story is based on a fragment of evidence which a correspondent calls the 'cryptic comment'. This is an annotation in pencil on a copy of the printed Prince Line Sailing Directions for 1908: 'Delete Italy due sale of *P. Prince* and *S. Prince* on stocks 1907'.

This raises interesting questions as to which yard was building the vessels intended to be named *Piedmontese Prince* and *Sardinian Prince* and were they to have two funnels? If the shipbuilder could be confirmed and the new owner found to be Italian, they might be the vessels I am postulating Prince Line were negotiating to charter.

Also to be considered are James Knott's political ambitions; he contested the 1906 election as a Conservative Party candidate in what was considered a safe seat. However, in this election a landslide swept the surprised Liberals into Parliament. Knott contested the next election in 1910 at Sunderland and this time was elected. As a prospective Parliamentary candidate and a local captain of industry he used the press for free publicity. The writer has never found any reference to a shipbuilding contract for the two emigrant ships.

The facts in chronological order are as follows:
In July 1906 a newspaper announces a three-ship order for Sir James Laing and Sons, Sunderland from Lloyd Sabaudo, Genoa
22nd December 1906: *Re d'Italia* launched
4th June 1907: last of the three ships, *Principe Di Pietmonte*, runs trials from the Tyne.
1907: fragmentary evidence of *Piedmontese Prince* and *Sardinian Prince* being sold on stocks
19th September 1908: in the weekly Prince Line fleet list published in Newcastle newspapers *Piedmontese Prince* and *Sardinian Prince* are both listed at Naples, the only time the ships are listed.
In conclusion, the newspaper report in 1906 of the Lloyd Sabaudo order for three ships definitely rules out the theory that these were Prince Line ships sold on the stocks. The tantalising annotation 'due sale of *P. Prince* and *S. Prince* on stocks 1907' is a confirmation that two ships were ordered, but what happened to them? Their names appearing in a 1908 fleet list does suggest a leak of information about a charter arrangement which was close but not finalised.

The author has searched local newspapers, which are an excellent source of news on shipping and shipbuilding. The only news items found are of the Lloyd Sabaudo order and the mention in the fleet list. Unless and until any further information is discovered, the matter remains a mystery. However, I hope the oft-quoted story about 'two funnel Prince Liners' will be suitably amended.

PRINCE LINE.
Roman Prince left the Mersey on the 17th
Syrian Prince arrived on the Syrian Coast on the 8th
Kaffir Prince arrived at London on the 17th
Carib Prince arrived at Sharpness on the 15th
Creole Prince arrived at Alexandria on the 13th
Moorish Prince arrived on the Syrian Coast on the 10th
Persian Prince passed Gravesend on the 13th
Grecian Prince left Santos on the 6th
Castilian Prince left San Francisco de Sul on the 17th
British Prince left Malta on the 15th
Imperial Prince left the Syrian Coast on the 14th
Highland Prince arrived on the Syrian Coast on the 3rd
Belgian Prince arrived in the Tyne on the 17th
Trojan Prince left the Mersey on the 17th
Corsican Prince left New York on the 10th
Egyptian Prince left the Syrian Coast on the 15th
Merchant Prince arrived at Bristol on the 14th
Sailor Prince left Alexandria on the 16th
Soldier Prince left Malta on the 17th
Italian Prince arrived at Santos on the 6th
Crown Prince left New York on the 15th
Saxon Prince left River Plate on the 15th
Norman Prince arrived at Santos on the 12th
Swedish Prince left New York on the 12th
Black Prince left Algiers on the 6th
Tudor Prince left New York on the 30th ult
Ocean Prince arrived at Santos on the 4th
African Prince arrived at Cape Town on the 16th
Afghan Prince arrived at New York on the 17th
Welsh Prince arrived at River Plate on the 9th
Royal Prince arrived at River Plate on the 9th ult
Norse Prince arrived at New Orleans on the 11th
Spanish Prince arrived at Middlesbrough on the 17th
Sicilian Prince at Naples
Napolitan Prince at Naples
Sardinian Prince at Naples
Piedmontese Prince at Naples
Russian Prince arrived in the Tyne on the 26th July
Mexican Prince arrived at Rouen on the 13th
Georgian Prince passed Pera on the 18th

The reference to *Piedmontese Prince* and *Sardinian Prince* in the 'Newcastle Daily Journal' for 19th September 1909. [Author]

248

Re d'Italia. *[Newall Dunn collection]*

Emigrant ships built by Laing for Lloyd Sabaudo, Genoa

RE D'ITALIA 1907-1929 Twin screw

5,204g 3,313n
430.0 x 52.7 x 25.0 feet
Two T. 3-cyl. (24, 39, 64 x 45 inches) by George Clark Ltd., Sunderland driving twin screws; 14 knots; four boilers, 180 psi.

22.12.1906: Launched by Sir James Laing and Sons, Sunderland (Yard No. 621) for Lloyd Sabaudo S.A. di Nav., Genoa, Italy as RE D'ITALIA.

3.1907: Completed.

6.4.1907: Commenced maiden voyage from Genoa to New York with calls at Naples and Palermo.

12.1908: Used as a hospital ship at Messina following an earthquake.

26.9.1911: Commenced a 14-month period as a hospital ship during the Italo-Turkish war. With 13 medical staff and accommodation for 116 patients she served between Italy and Libya and evacuated 36,983 sick and wounded.

1912: Made a single voyage to Constantinople.

1920: Accommodation reduced to first and third class only.

1921: Transferred to a South American service.

1929: Broken up at Genoa, where she had been laid up.

Photographs of the Lloyd Sabaudo ships are rare: this image of *Regina d'Italia* probably comes from a newspaper illustration. *[Collection of the late George Scott]*

REGINA D'ITALIA 1907-1928 Twin screw

5,204g 3,313n
430.0 x 52.7 x 25.0 feet
Two T. 3-cyl. (24, 39, 64 x 45 inches) by George Clark Ltd., Sunderland driving twin screws; 14 knots; four boilers, 180 psi.

21.1.1907: Launched by Sir James Laing and Sons, Sunderland (Yard No. 622) for Lloyd Sabaudo S.A. di Nav., Genoa, Italy as REGINA D'ITALIA.

4.1907: Completed.

15.5.1907: Commenced maiden voyage from Genoa to New York with calls at Naples and Palermo

6.10.1908: Inaugurated a service from Genoa to South America.

12.1908: Used as a hospital ship at Messina following an earthquake.

1911: Ran as a hospital ship between Benghazi and Derna during the Italo-Turkish war

1920: Accommodation reduced to first and third class only.

1921: Transferred to a South American service.

16.10.1928: Arrived at Genoa to be broken up.

Regina d'Italia. [Newall Dunn collection]

PRINCIPE DI PIEMONTE 1907-1914 Twin screw
5,365g 4,040n
430 x 52.7 x 25 feet
Two T. 3-cyl. (24, 39, 64 x 45 inches) by George Clark Ltd., Sunderland driving twin screws; 14 knots; four boilers, 180 psi.
1914: 60 second, 1,900 third passengers.
28.2.1907: Launched by Sir James

Laing and Sons Ltd., Sunderland (Yard No. 623) for Lloyd Sabaudo S.A. di Nav., Genoa as PRINCIPE DI PIEMONTE.
6.1907: Completed.
1.1914: Sold to Canadian Northern Steamships Ltd., Toronto.
12.2.1914: Transferred to Principello Steamships Ltd., Toronto (H.W. Harding, London, manager) as

PRINCIPELLO.
17.5.1916: Sold to the Cunard Steam Ship Co. Ltd., Liverpool and later renamed FOLIA.
11.3.1917: Torpedoed by the German submarine U 53 four miles east south east of Ram Head, County Waterford in position 51.51 north, 07.41 west whilst on a voyage from New York to Avonmouth with general cargo.

Principe di Piemonte. [Newall Dunn collection]

SCOTTISH STEAM OF THE PAST – NORTH SEA COASTERS

Graeme Somner

From the English border north of Berwick-on-Tweed to the most northerly Scottish port of Baltasound in the Shetland Islands, the Scottish east coast stretches some 300 miles. Ever since early times the inhabitants of this wild and rocky coastline have depended on boats and ships to bring them supplies of food, coal, cement, and fertilisers, taking away to the markets the produce of their labours such as grain, fish, potatoes, timber, stone and whisky. Despite the development of railways from the 1850s and later road transport, many small steamers continued to provide such services until the mid-1950s, when the cost of coal bunkers become prohibitive and steamers were gradually withdrawn and broken up. Their replacement by motor vessels met with only moderate success as trades had changed or disappeared, and now even the few such vessels remaining on the coastal trade are under threat.

The vessels latterly employed on this trade were ships of between 200 and 700 gross tons, capable of entering not only the major ports in the area, but also the many small ports dotted around the coastline, such as Kirkcaldy, Arbroath, Buckie, Lossiemouth, Inverness, Helmsdale, Invergordon, Wick, Stromness, Kirkwall, Scalloway, Lerwick and the farthest north of them all, Baltasound. They were usually engines-aft vessels, with either one or two holds, with a single derrick serving each hold, being rarely built for the trade but acquired second-hand at a knockdown price from other owners, usually at a ripe old age. The one-hold ships were usually fitted with a simple two-cylinder compound engine, whilst the larger vessels had the more efficient three-cylinder triple expansion engine.

In many cases at these small ports, be they docks or piers, there were no cranes or cargo handling equipment of any sort and the vessel's derrick was the only mechanical assistance available to discharge and load cargo. The ships had to have a relatively shallow draft as many ports did not have much depth of water even at high tide, and the vessel had to have the strength to lie on the harbour bottom at low water without damaging itself. They were crewed by a hardy breed of seaman who worked all hours at sea and in port, living in cramped, cold conditions, with many of them having to provide and cook their own food. The masters all came up the hard way having served on deck for many years and, often with little formal education or training, did nevertheless know the coast like the back of their hands, and could somehow 'smell' the way through tricky channels in thick weather – there was no radar in the early days. Some had echometers indicating the depth of water under the keel, and the odd ship even had a radio telephone, but generally that was all.

All this has now gone some fifty years ago and to-day we can look back with nothing but admiration for the efforts of the steamers and crews who worked the coastal trades through this period.

Single-hold steamers

Archallan was of 235 tons gross, and had been built at Paisley for a Glasgow ship owner in 1900 as *Ferrum*. In 1911 she was bought by Newcastle owners when her original measurements gave her a gross tonnage of 271 and a net of only 19. This allowed her to trade to the Thames without paying dues, and also gave certain concessions at other ports such as Berwick-on-Tweed, but it was not long before the Board of Trade decided that the tonnage was a freak figure and made alterations to the calculations, so that

Archallan in Sheves' funnel colours of black with a red band. *[W.H. Brown/Author's collection]*

Wisbech discharging coal at Kirkwall. *[Author's collection]*

her official net tonnage became 89. This change, however, still gave her owners some benefits in dues. She moved back to Wales and the west coast of England in 1919. She was renamed *Eddie* in 1938, before being employed on the sand trade in the River Tay in 1939. In May 1943 she was acquired by Gordon A. Sheves of Fraserburgh and initially employed carrying coal for the Royal Navy to Scapa Flow. She moved on to other trades later in the war and on 10th December 1944, whilst on passage from Hull to Middlesbrough with a cargo of steel, sent out a distress call when her cargo shifted in heavy weather. She made her way to nearby Bridlington, Yorkshire under her own power where the cargo was reloaded. When regulations permitted in 1945,

she was renamed *Archallan* and was to be seen in many Scottish minor ports. She was sold in 1951 to Newcastle owners, and arrived for breaking up at Dunston-on-Tyne on 6th April 1953, with 53 years of service behind her.

Wisbech of 219 tons gross, was built during 1916 in Yorkshire, originally named *JWN* for Hull owners. She was fitted with two masts and is seen at Kirkwall discharging coal on to lorries using iron buckets. She had been renamed *Wisbech* in 1932 and after going through the hands of various English owners, was bought by the Tay Sand Co. Ltd. of Dundee for service as a sand dredger. She was relieved of this mundane task in February 1943 when every available ship was needed for the war effort, and acquired by Bremner

Orkney Dawn at Stromness, Orkney loaded with barrels. *[Johny Towers/Author's collection]*

and Company of Kirkwall to supply the needs of the Royal Navy and northern islanders. This service she carried out until April 1953 when she returned to sand dredging in the Tay. She went to the breakers at St David's-on-Forth in June 1960 with a respectable 44 years of service behind her.

Orkney Dawn of 345 tons gross was built in Beverley, Yorkshire in 1921 as *Redesmere* for trading on the west coast of England. Unusually for such a small ship she was fitted with a triple-expansion engine of 73 nominal horsepower instead of the compound engine which was standard for a vessel of her type. She became *Brockley Combe* of Bristol in 1926. In February 1937 she was acquired by George Couper and Co. Ltd. of Helmsdale, Sutherland, renamed *Lothdale* and was generally employed in carrying coal north to the Orkney and Shetland Islands and taking her owner's fish products (he was a trawler owner as well) to markets in the south. She took the name *Orkney Dawn* in February 1953 when she was sold to Bremner and Company of Kirkwall in the Orkney Islands and is seen here at Stromness (in the Orkneys) loaded with wooden casks – for the whisky trade, one wonders? Her time in northern waters was short as in August 1955 she was sold to owners based at Whitehaven, and renamed *Cumbria*. She arrived at Troon, Ayrshire for breaking up on 3rd July 1957, a mere 31 years old.

Denwick Head of 265 tons gross was yet another of the many small coasters built in the 1920s. Launched in 1923 at Bideford, Devon she was owned by the well-known millers, Spillers. She was acquired by the Leith firm of A.F. Henry and MacGregor Ltd. in 1933 and carried such cargoes as coal, fertilisers and salted fish. She is seen on 25th July 1938 discharging (probably fertilisers in bags) on to horse carts in the Albert Basin at Leith. The 'London boat' on the General Steam Navigation berth is *Groningen* (1,205/1928) loading for the mid-week London departure. Note the fact that, despite crane and rail facilities being readily

available, ship's gear and horse drawn transport are being used. *Denwick Head* was sold to west of Scotland owners in March 1946 and traded in the Western Isles until arriving at shipbreaking yard at Glasgow in July 1955, a youngster of 32 years.

Two-hold steamers

Dunmoir started life as the London-registered *Steersman* in 1909. Of 562 tons gross, she was built on the Tyne with a larger than traditional number 1 hold to permit long lengths of steel or timber to be carried. After being renamed *Continental Trader* and then *Lowick*, she was acquired in May 1936 by Buchan and Hogg of Grangemouth and renamed *Dunmoir*. She was mainly employed on the firm's regular service between Grangemouth and London, but during the Second World War found herself in many small and unusual ports, such as in the autumn of 1939 at the Moray Firth harbour of Macduff discharging coal. She remained in service until July 1954 when she arrived at Antwerp, Belgium for breaking up, having given a total of 43 years of service.

Archgrove of 602 tons gross was a typical Glasgow coaster of the period, built in 1894 on the Clyde for the well-known owner William Robertson as *Citrine*. After sale to Langlands of Glasgow for whom she worked as *Princess Thyra*, she was re-acquired by Robertson in 1905 and renamed *Bronzite*. She was purchased by Gordon A. Sheves of Fraserburgh in August 1946 to be employed carrying coal from north-east English ports to northern Scotland (or any other trade her owner could find). She had an unfortunate history of being involved in collisions – on 28th July 1948 with the Swedish steamer *Stureborg* (2,358/1918) off Harwich, Suffolk, whilst carrying cement from London to Alloa; on 28th January 1949 with the steamer *Afon Morlais* (965/1944) in the North Sea while on passage from Plymouth to the Tyne in ballast, and again on 23rd April

Denwick Head uses her single derrick to discharge at Leith on 25th July 1938. *[W.J. Allan/Author's collection]*

Dunmoir lying at Grangemouth in 1953. Note the particularly long well deck. *[Author's collection]*

Archgrove. Her wheelhouse was probably fitted during the Second World War and her mizzen mast removed at the same time. *[Author's collection]*

1949 in the River Thames with the Leith steamer *Benvenue* (7,846/1948). Her final voyage brought her to Antwerp, Belgium to meet the shipbreaker's torch on 5th December 1957, a well-worn 63-year-old.

Cantick Head was one of the extensive fleet of A.F. Henry and MacGregor Ltd. of Leith. Built in 1921 at Aberdeen for the General Steam Navigation Co. Ltd.t of London as *Oriole*, her gross tonnage was 488 tons. It was not until June 1938 that her name changed to *Cantick Head* and she became employed carrying road stone south bound for southern English ports, returning from the River Thames with bagged cement to Scottish ports anywhere between Berwick upon Tweed and Lerwick – the company were the chief distributors of Blue Circle cement in Scotland. She survived the Second World War unscathed except for slight

damage when a German bomber attacked her off Kinnaird Head, Aberdeenshire on 11th February 1941. She was sold after 17 years of service to Liverpool owners and became *Bannspur*, finally arrived at Dublin for breaking up on 8th October 1960 – a good innings of 39 years.

Barra Head, slightly larger at 671 tons gross, joined the fleet of Henry and MacGregor in 1931. She had been built at Goole just over a year earlier for South Wales owners as *Portavon*. Employed carrying road stone south, cement north like the rest of the fleet, she was however restricted because of her length to serving the larger Scottish ports, such as Leith, Aberdeen and Inverness. She too survived the Second World War without a scratch despite the fact she sailed in many convoys up and down the East coast – of the fleet of 12 at the beginning of the war, the company

Cantick Head in 1952, probably in the Thames. *[W.H. Brown/Author's collection]*

was to suffer the loss of five vessels. She continued to work for Henry and MacGregor until the pending opening in 1963 of the cement works (the first one in Scotland) at Dunbar, East Lothian, as a result of which the cement trade from the south would virtually disappear, resulting in her early demise. She arrived at Grangemouth for breaking up on 23rd August 1961, having completed 30 years in service.

Postscript

As a school boy I myself made a voyage on *Barra Head* in the summer of 1936. I joined the vessel at Inverkeithing, Fife where she was just completing loading one thousand tons of road stone. Captain MacMillan welcomed me aboard and showed me my quarters – the designated second mate's cabin (they didn't carry one!) located just under the bridge on the starboard side, next door to the chart room.

I signed on as captain's steward at one shilling (10p) a month, and paid the cook/steward the princely sum of 2/6d (25p) per day for my food. I would eat with the master and mate (who, incidentally, had only one eye) in the saloon immediately underneath me.

We sailed on the tide late that evening bound for Ipswich, the weather being calm with little wind. All went well until when, approaching Great Yarmouth, Norfolk in the early hours of our second day at sea, we ran into fog. The engine speed was brought down to 'slow', the steam whistle was sounded at the regulation interval of one minute, and a lookout stationed in the bow – not that he could see much as visibility was less than 200 feet. With the master on the bridge at the wheel, we crept through the murk hearing other whistle sounds round about us – fortunately Captain MacMillan had earlier decided to take the outer (and longer)

Barra Head heading north with a full cargo. *[Fotoflite incorporating Skyfotos/Author's collection]*

passage past Great Yarmouth so as to meet less traffic. Nothing of note was encountered until 1.00 a.m. when two high pitched whistles were heard dead ahead – Captain MacMillan thought they were probably a pair of Dutch trawlers fishing with a net between them despite the weather. Speed was reduced to 'dead slow' and after some minutes we sighted two trawlers close under our port bow happily trawling away, having fortunately just passed in front of us. The fog later lifted and we approached Harwich in daylight and made our way up the River Orwell to Ipswich Dock, some eleven miles from the North Sea. Discharge of our cargo commenced immediately and on the following morning we were ready to catch the morning tide and head for the River Thames and yet another cargo of bagged cement.

There was one fly in the ointment, however. On an adjacent berth astern of us there was another similar-sized coaster discharging stone from Wales and Captain MacMillan knew that she too was bound for the Thames, where the order of loading was 'first come, first served'. Captain MacMillan was determined to be first in the queue and during the late evening lowered the ship's dinghy and had a rope passed from our bow to a bollard at the dock entrance, so as to be able to pull his bow out of the berth and into the lock. In doing so the rope prevented the Welsh coaster astern of us getting out of her berth, as she had to carry out the same movement to get to the lock. It worked! Out of the dock we went in the dawn with the 'Taffy' close behind us and we were both soon back in the North Sea. Being light and drawing the minimum of water, Captain MacMillan decided to come out of the marked channel after passing Harwich and take a short cut south. 'Taffy' did the same but we had the edge on speed and the distance between us steadily increased. We arrived in the Thames and dropped our anchor off Swanscombe, Kent to await instructions to go alongside a wharf to load bags of cement.

Captain MacMillan was told that loading would not be commencing until the next day, so the dinghy was launched to take him ashore so that he could travel on ship's business to the Customs House, next to the Tower of London. I went with him for the experience of going to 'the Big Smoke'.

Next day we were called to go alongside a wharf where bags of cement from a works some distance away were brought to us by a light railway – the cement was obviously newly manufactured as the contents of the bags were still warm. We loaded something like 1,000 tons of cement, nicely stacked in the two holds, for Aberdeen and Inverness and sailed the next day. Our 'Taffy' friend from Ipswich was still lying at anchor awaiting his turn to load. The rope had saved the day.

All went well until we passed Great Yarmouth when we ran into a very strong north-westerly gale (until then we had been sheltered by land). Although my cabin was under the bridge, water was passing by my door, and the ship's movement was fairly violent. We continued heading north into the short seas of the North Sea and during the early hours of next day were some miles off the Tyne when the chief engineer reported that the engine condenser had failed. Speed had to be reduced to a crawl to conserve fresh water and Captain MacMillan decided to make for Blyth, just north of the Tyne, where the owners had an agent. On his radio telephone he called Blyth for a pilot but failed to get an answer. Committed to make port at Blyth he pressed on and just outside Blyth started sounding his whistle for a pilot. It was nearly an hour before the pilot boat appeared, and even when the pilot got aboard at 6.00 a.m. he thought he was bringing in the *Cantick Head*, which was expected at Blyth to load coal! Later that morning the hatch covers were taken off to see how the cargo had been affected by the rough weather. The nicely piled bags of cement that had left the Thames were found to be in disarray and would have to be re-stowed before the voyage could continue. My voyage, however, was to end at Blyth as repairs were going to take several days, and so I went home to Edinburgh by rail via Newcastle.

PUTTING THE RECORD STRAIGHT

Letters, additions, amendments and photographs relating to features in any issues of 'Record' are welcomed. Letters may be lightly edited. Note that comments on multi-part articles are consolidated and included in the issue of 'Record' following the final part. Senders of e-mails are asked to include their postal address.

Who killed British shipbuilding?
I wonder if I may be allowed to comment on a remark in the latest Ships in Focus 'Record' (issue 47): 'Some may be beginning to believe that the unions were not entirely to blame for the closure of British shipyards'. My family worked for four generations as boilermakers in the Tees shipyards. As someone who was shop steward and eventually convenor for 15 years at Smith's Dock between

1960 and 1976, I obviously have some experience and opinions on the subject.

During the 15 years and for many years before my involvement with the union, there was not one strike by the boilermakers at Smith's Dock. Any new equipment introduced to improve efficiency and cut costs was accepted and because of the flexibility between boilermaking trades the 'who twangs the string' kind of stoppage that the press loved so much did not happen. During these years Smith's Dock was as profitable as any other yard and more so than most; at this time our wages were the highest on the north east coast. The management must be given credit for this. They treated their employees as part of the team not as a necessary evil. The 'them and us' attitude, which was common in most yards, went a long

way towards the bad industrial relations that existed elsewhere. In a recent television programme about the closure of the Clyde yards, Mr Stephens of the Alexander Stephens yard admitted that the hire and fire system adopted by most yard managements did not create any feeling of loyalty amongst the work force and made very difficult the introduction of new, more efficient equipment that would cause redundancies. The Smith's Dock management response to a run down of shipbuilding was to take on extra ship repair work to keep as many men as possible employed. Teesside had industries other than shipyards that always needed boilermakers. This meant that tradesmen were not just waiting to be called back when needed.

Swan Hunter took over Smith's Dock but the higher wages at Smith's prevented a total amalgamation and we were left to run ourselves as before. Any profits being made by us were taken at the year end to help other yards in the group. Swan Hunter later appointed one of their men, a Mr Parker, to be Managing Director at Smith's. He was a typical Scotch-type gaffer who expressed surprise in the books he wrote later at the good labour relationship and at the very high level of production that there was at Smith's Dock before he arrived. His attitude towards the employees was totally at odds with what we had been accustomed to in the past and most certainly made us realise what men had to put up with in most other yards.

In 1990, two years after the yard closed, life-long Smith's Dock man Roger Spence (who also had been Managing Director) gave a talk on the history of the yard. He said that at the time the order came to close the yard it was equipped with the most modern systems available, had an excellent workforce and plenty of firm inquiries for orders. The government changed the credit facilities for new ships from that which prevailed throughout Europe to one that offered half the time to pay for a ship at twice the previous interest level. This of course made it impossible to compete with other, better-financed yards in Europe and closed the yard.

Who was to blame? Was it the yard owners who would not modernise after the war because they would have lost some of the lucrative time and material orders that were there? Was it the unions for responding in the same manner to the poor treatment they received in most yards? Or was it a government who at that time seemed to be determined to close any manufacturing industry that had strong unions?
BILL BLACKWELL, 101 Staithes Lane, Staithes, Saltburn, Cleveland.

Before and after sludge disposal

Recently I came across an obituary notice for Captain Henry Rockett of Salford, who was master of the Manchester Corporation steamer *Joseph Thompson* for some years ('Record' 47). He died aged 53 on the 15th June 1908.

The obituary noted that Henry Rocket was formerly master of the steamer *Pioneer* owned by the Cooperative Wholesale Society Ltd. when in 1894 it was the first cargo ship to navigate the full length of the Manchester Ship Canal.
TED GRAY, 28 Queen's Valley, Ramsey, Isle of Man IM8 1NG

These photographs of *Joseph Thompson* berthed at the sewage treatment works at Davyhulme are believed to date from around 1926. *[Ted Gray collection]*

Regarding your article in 'Record' 47 questioning the fate of the *Olympic*, ex-*Percy Dawson*. I can confirm it is still sailing as a water tanker between Rhodes and neighbouring islands. I photographed her off Rhodes on 3rd June 2010.
COLIN LEONARD, Runcorn WA7 5SB
Craig Osbourne tells us that one of the photographs of Shieldhall *on page 187 of 'Record' 47 has been printed back to front. Ed.*

More on British Shipowners Co. Ltd.

I was pleased to see the article on British Shipowners Co. Ltd. in 'Record' 45. I can fill some gaps in their careers from the British Shipbuilding Database. *Nelson* was launched 1.8.1862 (it is not uncommon to find launch dates a week apart, as some publications reported 'last Wednesday' but held the item over to the following week).
British Sovereign was launched 13.10.1864.
British Nation was launched 28.3.1865. She was yard number 8.
British Viceroy was launched 27.12.1864. The builder was Union Shipbuilding Company.
British Envoy was launched 28.4.1866.
British Flag was launched 29.7.1866. She was yard number 197.
British Consul was launched 4.8.1866.
British Admiral was launched 9.3.1867. She was yard number 198.
British Statesman was launched 6.4.1867.
British Navy was yard number 243.
British Commodore was built as *Knight Bachelor*.
British Army was launched 4.9.1869. Her initial port of registry was Newcastle.

British Ambassador was launched 12.8.1873.

British Admiral was launched 22.11.1873.

The Bruce. Her builder was Aitken and Mansel (not Mansell) and her yard number 25.

British Isles. I think later names as lighters were TIGRE and OCEANIA. She survived into the 1950S.

IAN BUXTON, 12 Grand Parade, Tynemouth, North Shields, Tyne and Wear NE30 4JS

Bains, brigantines and barquentines

I read with great interest the article on Portreath and the Bains ('Record' 47). The sailing vessel list mistakenly has the *Penwith* as an iron brigantine, while as mentioned in the text and illustrated she was a barquentine. The following vessels are also listed as iron brigantines (formerly of different rig): *Thomas Blythe* and *Penair* (both listed as ships in 'Lloyd's Register' for 1877-78), and *Belle of Lagos* (listed as a barque in 'Lloyd's Register' of 1877-1878).

Lloyd's Register was slow to accept the term barquentine though it does appear in the 1877-1878 register book. Perhaps it depended on just how up to date the surveyor was. I suggest the above vessels were probably also barquentines - it would seem unnecessarily expensive converting iron three-masted vessels to two-masted vessels.

Several years ago I researched the 'brigantine' *Royal Harrie*, mainly because at 501 gross tons I thought her exceptionally large for the rig. Only when I located a painting of the vessel did I find out she was a barquentine. 'Lloyd's Register' sometimes used 'Bn' for brigantine plus an annotation 'three masts' in lieu of the term barquentine.

CAPTAIN JOHN ANDERSON, 523 Louise Road, Ladysmith, British Columbia, Canada V9G 1W7.

I have one tiny observation on the list of sailing ships on page172 of 'Record' 47. The third of them – *English Maid* – is noted as having been built by the Peterhead Shipbuilding Company of Perth. I know nothing of the small nineteenth century shipbuilding enterprises in either Peterhead or Perth but I am surprised that a small Peterhead company in 1856 should have had an offshoot 100 miles away at Perth. I wondered whether the name of the building company was perhaps correct whereas the location had been mis-transcribed from an abbreviated version of Peterhead.

COLIN MENZIES, London W1U 6BP

Bain's third steamer, the 1869-built *Lynx*, was in the fleet from 1893 until her loss in 1899. This photograph strongly suggests she is the steamer seen to the right of *Coniston Fell* in the upper photograph on page 179 of 'Record' 47, although in the above photograph the gaff on her foremast is not visible. *Lynx* and *Coniston Fell* were in the fleet together from 1895 to 1899. *[Ian Wilson collection]*

Ian Wilson has also kindly supplied photographs of the German motor coaster *Kondor* making one of the last visits by a ship to Portreath. Of the four coasters to carry this name in post-war years, only the 1952-built, 278-gross *Kondor* was registered at Schulau. This would date the photograph to between 1962 and 1965, when she was owned by Walter Hintz of Schulau. *[Ian Wilson collection]*

BOSUN'S LOCKER

It never ceases to amaze us how knowledgeable our readers are. There was so little to work from in the photos in our last issue but again you came up trumps with three of them. As for the other three, in the course of time, someone may stumble a across the photos elsewhere and then we will have the answers. There is the expression 'many hands make light work', perhaps with the Bosun's Locker it should be 'many eyes identify picture'. If you come up with an answer six months, or even six years after we published trhe photo we would still like to hear.

Identification of photographs in 'Record' 47

Identifying the wrecks at Normandy proved a tough challenge, and only Chris F. Kleiss has come up with a positive identification. He has a postcard taken from a different angle which establishes that 47/02 shows the *Aaro* (1,426/1925). This Danish ship, built at Helsingør for local company A/S D/S Heimdal (hence the letter 'H' on her funnel), had arrived in Liverpool in May 1940 and was subsequently requisitioned by the British Ministry of War Transport. Off Omaha Beach during a gale on 6th October 1944, *Aaro* dragged her anchor, was beached and became a total loss after collision with the steamers *Lysland* (1,335/1937) and *Yewdale* (823/1929).

Examination of 47/03 suggests this photograph was taken long after the war: several of those on board, including several ladies, are in swimming costumes!

Thanks also to Richard Pryde and Tony Smith for their thoughts.

47/04

Correspondents suggest the Holland Amerika ship is either the *Nieuw Amsterdam* of 1906 or the *Rotterdam* of 1908, both built by Harland and Wolff at Belfast. Although most of those who wrote favoured the *Rotterdam*, reference to Arnold Kludas' 'Great Passenger Ships of the World', volume 1, leaves no doubt that it is the *Nieuw Amsterdam*, which had four masts, *Rotterdam* having just two. It is possible that the way the photographs in the Kludas book are laid out, with the ships appearing in reverse order to when they were built, might have caused some confusion. Photograph 47/04 was taken after 1910 when the fore end of the promenade deck of the *Nieuw Amsterdam*, originally open, was enclosed with glass windows (the *Rotterdam* had this feature from new). Tony Smythe notes that *Nieuw Amsterdam* maintained a skeleton service between the Netherlands and New York during the First World War, and was demoted to cabin class only in the late 1920s. She was broken up at Osaka in 1932. Thanks also to M.J. Bamforth, Geoff Holmes, Archie Munro, Richard Pryde and W.G. Tremlett for their suggestions.

47/06

There is no doubt that the ship in this French photograph started life as either the *Heliopolis* of 1907 or the *Cairo* of 1908, sisters completed by Fairfield for the short lived and unprofitable service between Marseille and Alexandria of Egyptian Mail Steamship Co. Ltd. of London. They were triple-screw, turbine-driven ships capable of 30 knots. Sold in 1910 to Canadian Northern Steamships Ltd., Toronto they were renamed *Royal George* and *Royal Edward* respectively for their new owners Avonmouth to Montreal service (see 'Record' 18). Both ships became troop transports in 1914 and both Canadian Northern and its *Royal George* were bought by Cunard in 1916, the ship being broken up at Wilhelmshaven in 1922. *Royal Edward* was torpedoed and sunk by UB 14 in the Aegean Sea on 13th August 1915. She was sailing unescorted from Alexandra to Mudros, and of 1,366 troops and 220 crew on board, fewer than 500 survived.

It is not so easy to decide which of the two ships is shown. On page 139 of 'Great Passenger Ships of the World' (Volume 1), Arnold Kludas has included photographs labelled as *Heliopolis* and *Cairo* which reveal two distinct differences between the ships. The *Heliopolis* had a deck house behind the bridge on the boat deck which extended well aft of the forward funnel; that in *Cairo* was much shorter. The *Heliopolis* photograph also shows that she had considerably taller ventilators on the boat deck. As built the pair had what is described as silver-grey hulls and all-yellow funnels, and although the hull remained grey for Canadian Northern, the funnels of *Royal Edward* and *Royal George* were given red tops. The funnel in 47/06 certainly could be yellow and has no coloured top. This would strongly suggest that photograph 47/06, which was taken in Marseilles, shows *Cairo* as running from that port to Alexandria for Egyptian Mail.

However, there is a catch. Peter Newall, who has researched these ships, points out that they were notoriously bad for rolling, and that the structures on the boat deck were reduced to help counter this tendency. The photographs on page 81 of 'Record' 18 show that, in Canadian Northern days, there were no discernible differences in lengths of deckhouse or heights of ventilator. It could just be that the shots on page 81 are actually of the same ship (publicity shots were often altered, or just wrongly labelled) but other photographs of *Royal Edward* and *Royal George* confirm that they became identical. From information on the back of photograph 47/06 the sender was on active service, so it may well date from the First World War, by when the livery had probably been altered. If so it could show either *Royal Edward* or *Royal George*, which just happened to call at Marseilles on a trooping voyage. The balance of probability, however, is that 47/06 shows the ship as *Cairo*.

Again, thanks for help with this problem to Geoff Holmes, Archie Munro, Peter Newall, Richard Pryde, and W.G. Tremlett and especially to Tony Smythe John H. Wilterding who identified differences between *Heliopolis* and *Cairo*.

48/01. A fine picture of what appears to be a British India steamer at Malta. A look through Laxon and Perry's book on B.I. is of little help, in fact, it makes one wonder if she is a B.I. ship as so few of the vessels illustrated from this era appear to have two funnels. Although un-identifiable the next ship back is a Hain vessel and protruding from the line-up there is what could be another of the company's ships. The photograph has nothing on the back.

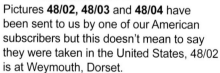

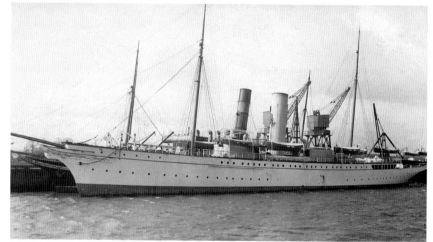

Pictures **48/02**, **48/03** and **48/04** have been sent to us by one of our American subscribers but this doesn't mean to say they were taken in the United States, 48/02 is at Weymouth, Dorset.

48/02. What is the two funnelled steamer in the foreground (top)? The Hain vessel behind her is the *Trevanion* which was in their fleet from 1891 through to 1916 when she disappeared.

48/03. The name on the bow is *Excellent* and crudely painted on her side *SS Excellent* (above). But what is happening? She is blowing off much steam and on the left there is what may be a large warship, her decks lined with bystanders. A mooring line is draped around her bow and the falls of a lifeboat on her stern are almost down to the water.

48/04. This could be *Varuna* but can anyone confirm this (middle right)?

48/05. Black funnel, black hull, not much to help in identifying her but the broken back may lead to a result (bottom right).

INDEX TO RECORD 45 TO 48
Issue numbers are shown in bold

Re d'Italia (1907) **48**:248-9
Redesmere (1921) **48**:253
Regina d'Italia (1907)
48:249-50
Rei de Portugal (1889) **48**:247
Reinholt **45**:51
Renata (1983) **46**:98
Resolve (1960) **48**:203
Rhexenor **48**:232
Rio Conquista (1979) **46**:98
Rio Daule (1968) **47**:157
Rio Santa Rosa (1972) **48**:237
Ripon Victory (1945) **46**:87
Rippingham Grange **48**:233
Rita 1 (1953) **46**:103
Robin Hood **45**:10
Rodrigo (1983) **46**:98
Rogate **45**:21
Roman Hurricane (1973)
48:240
Roman Reefer **48**:234
Rong Ning 82 (1983) **46**:98
Rosalie Moller **45**:48
Roseville **45**:50
Rotterdam (1878) **46**:111,115
Rotterdam (1908) **48**:259
Rouen (1888) **48**:208-9
Rouen (1912) **48**:209,214-5
Royal Edward (1908) **48**:259
Royal George (1907) **48**:259
Royal Harrie (barquentine)
48:258
Rubonia **46**:118
Rupert de Larrinaga **46**:98
Ryong Gang 2 (1980) **46**:97
Ryu Gyong (1983) **46**:98
S. Lucia (1968) **47**:156
Safmarine Namibe (1983)
46:98
Sagamore (1893)
45:60-2,**46**:99
Saigon 3 (1980) **46**:97
Saigon 5 (1980) **46**:97
Saint Agnes (1) (1865) **47**:172
Saint Agnes (2) (1872) **47**:172
Saint Francis (1948) **46**:102
Sainte Marguerite II (1921?)
47:169
Sakae Maru **45**:27
Sakaye Maru **45**:27
Salaga (1947) **47**:138
Salford (1895) **47**:129,182
Salford City (1928) **47**:182-4
Salinas (1972) **48**:237
Salmara (1956)
46:68,76-7,**47**:189
Salsette (1956) **46**:68,76
Samaria (1921) **45**:34
Samarovsk **45**:23
Saminver **45**:22
Samphill **45**:22
Samsperrin **45**:22
Samvern **45**:22
Samyale (1943) **47**:134
San Francisco Borja (1952)
46:126
San Georgio III (1961) **48**:204
Sandsend **45**:22
Sangara (1939) **47**:131,144
Sannio (1899) **46**:114,118
Sansu **47**:130-1,144-5
Santa Ana (1949) **46**:69
Santa Suria (1977) **47**:152
Santa Vassiliki (1971) **46**:97
Sapporo Maru No. 11 **45**:27
Sarah Fox (1868) **47**:172
Sarangani Bay
(Sardinian Prince) **48**:247-8
Satsuma (1901) **45**:45
Scale Force (1883) **47**:181
Scapwind (1970) **46**:97
Sea Lion (1977) **46**:97

Sea Moon (1967) **46**:91
Sea Union **45**:50
Sea Venture (1972) **46**:97
Seaboard Costa Rica **46**:94
Seaforth **47**:131
Seeadler **45**:18
Seine (1891) **48**:208-9
Seki Roanoke **46**:94
Sekondi (1948) **47**:139
Sem Jong (1982) **46**:97
Seydlitz **45**:63
Shahristan **45**:50
Shanghai Pride (1983) **46**:98
Shankara (1956) **46**:104
Shankara Jayanti **46**:104
Sheepshead Bay Victory
(1945) **46**:71
Shellphalte (1952) **45**:42-4
Sherbro (1947) **47**:132,136
Shieldhall (1910)
47:184,187,**48**:257
Shillong (1949) **46**:68,74
Shimosa (1902) **45**:45
Shipinco I **46**:98
Shonga (1947) **47**:137
Shoreham **45**:59
Shropshire (1959) **48**:197
Shun King **46**:70
Sicilian Prince (1889) **48**:247
Sierra Nevada (1972) **47**:165
Sijilmassa (1972) **47**:163
Siltonhall (1958) **46**:118
Silveravon (1977) **47**:146
Silverbriar **45**:55
Silverbum (1953) **46**:109
Silverdee **47**:146
Silverforce (1957) **46**:109
Silverlake (1958) **46**:109
Silverlaurel (1950)
45:53;**46**:87
Silverplane **45**:55
Silversandal **45**:53
Simeto (1944) **47**:133
Singapore (1951) **46**:68,75
Sirius **45**:19
Sithonia (1942) **47**:145
Skegness **45**:27
Skiathos Reefer (1970) **47**:159
Skogland **45**:28
Skudefjord **45**:28
Slevik (1969) **47**:158
Slieve Bawn **45**:12
Slieve More **45**:12
Smara (1971) **47**:160
Sneaton **45**:22
Sobo **47**:131
Socotra (1943)
46:66-7,69,**47**:188
Sofia **46**:121
Solideo (1893) **45**:61-2
Somali (1948) **46**:68,73
Song Duong (1979) **46**:97
Sorabjee Jamsetjee
Jeejeebhoy **45**:11,15
Sotrudnik (1896) **46**:118
Soudan (1948) **46**:67-8,71-3
South Africa Star **48**:234
South Islands (1986) **46**:96-7
Spartan Prince (1897) **48**:247
Sperrbrecher 14 **45**:46
Spring (1979) **46**:97
Spyros (1952) **46**:104
St. Denis (1895) **46**:121
Staffordshire **45**:19
Stalo (1953) **46**:108
Stanhall (1925) **45**:47-8
Stanholme (1945) **46**:71
Stanmore (1945) **46**:70
Star 3 (1981) **46**:98
Star of the East **45**:10
Steersman (1909) **48**:253
Stella Fairy (1984) **47**:162

Stephanos Vergottis (1973)
46:97
Sto. Nino (1954) **46**:126
Storm Nymph (1854) **47**:171-2
Strathardle (1967) **46**:68,78
Strathbrora (1967) **46**:68,79
Strathconon (1967)
46:66,68,79
Strathlomond (1956) **46**:75
Strathloyal (1956)
46:77,**47**:189
Stromness **45**:27
Sturdy Falcon (1980) **46**:97
Stureborg (1918) **48**:253
Suerte **45**:9
Sulima (1948) **47**:134,140
Sully (1874) **47**:178
Sunbaden (1970) **47**:149
Sunda (1952) **46**:65,68,75
Sunderland Venture (1985)
46:95,97
Sunnyville **45**:50
Suntempest (1969) **46**:89
Surat (1948) **46**:68,73
Suruga (1908) **45**:45
Sussex Trader (1947) **46**:106
Swedru (1) (1937) **47**:131
Swedru (2) (1948) **47**:141
Tagaytay **45**:50,53
Tagus (1953) **45**:50;**46**:92
Tai Fong (1951) **46**:108
Tai Ping (1958) **45**:46,50;**46**:94
Tai Shan **45**:46
Tai Yang **45**:46
Tai Yin **45**:46
Taiko (1968) **45**:50,53
Taimyr **45**:50-1;**46**:86
Tairea (1956) **46**:75
Takoradi **45**:51;**46**:94
Talabot (1967) **45**:50, **46**:86
Talabot (1979) **46**:93
Talisman (1977) **45**:53;**46**:93
Talthybius **45**:53
Tamano **46**:86
Tamara **45**:52
Tamele (1944) **47**:130
Tamerlane **45**:50,53
Tamil Periyar E.V.R (1957)
46:107
Tamise (1893) **48**:208-9
Tampa **45**:50-1;**46**:91;**47**:189
Tamworth (1924) **48**:213
Tanea (1950) **45**:38-9,44
Tantalus **45**:53
Tarantel **45**:50,53
Tariq (1971) **47**:187
Tarkwa (1944) **47**:130
Taronga (1967) **45**:50,53;**46**:91
Tartar Prince (1895) **48**:247
Tasneem (1952) **46**:108
Taurus **45**:46
Teesside Clipper (1972) **48**:238
Teesta (1956) **46**:77;**47**:189
Teiresias **45**:53
Telamon (1950) **45**:53;**46**:87
Telemachus **45**:53
Tema (1959) **45**:49-51
Tema (ro-ro) (1984) **45**:51
Temeraire **45**:50,53
Tennessee (1977) **45**:50,53
Tephys **46**:98
Tercia (1866) **45**:15
Terrier (1977) **45**:53-4
Test (1890) **47**:176,181
Teucer (1950) **45**:53;**46**:87
Teviot, HMS **48**:215
Texas (1961)
45:50,**46**:86,**47**:189
Thai Binh (1980) **46**:97
Thala Dan **48**:225,235
The Bruce (1866)
45:11,16,**48**:258

The Queen (1903)
48:208,213-4
Theben (1953) **45**:50;**46**:92
Themis (1954) **45**:50,53;:91
Theodor Korner (1975) **48**:244
Theofilos (1985) **46**:95,97
Thermopylae (1977) **45**:53
Thetis **46**:98
Thistle Venture (1966)
45:4;**46**:81
Thistledowne (1953) **46**:107
Thomas Blythe (1859)
47:171-2;**48**:258
Thomas K (1953) **46**:108
Thurland Castle (1929) **45**:48
(Thurland Castle) (1951)
45:48,53
Tia Yang **45**:46
Tian Mu Shan **47**:159
Tigre (1884) **48**:258
Tijuca (1959) **45**:49-51;**46**:86
Tilapa (1928) **47**:144
Timur Girl (1973) **47**:166
Tina (1964) **46**:98
Tina 2 (1979) **46**:98
Tirranna **45**:50,53
Titan **45**:20
Titania (1958)
45:47,50,**46**:85,94
To Lich (1980) **46**:97
Tonghai **45**:52
Toreador (1954) **45**:50
Torrens (1972) **47**:163
Tortugas **45**:50
Tough Trader (1980) **46**:97
Towada (1953) **46**:92
Toyo (1954) **46**:91
Trade Grace (1977) **47**:146
Travancore **45**:52
Traviata (1959) **45**:49-50,53
Tregea (1872) **47**:171-2
Trelawny (1949) **46**:102
Treleigh (1894) **47**:173-8
Trenchant (HM submarine)
45:32
Trentbank **48**:234
Trevanion (1891) **48**:260
Trinidad (1968)
45:50,53;**46**:86
Trio (1861) **47**:172
Troja **45**:46
Trojan Prince (1896) **48**:247
Trojan Star (1973) **48**:240
Tropical Breeze (1972)
48:237
Trouncer (HMS) (1943)
45:48;**46**:89
Tsu (1977) **45**:53
Tucurui (1988) **46**:98
Tugela (1954) **45**:50-1
Tungfong (1950) **46**:124
Turandot (1957) **45**:50
Tuscan Star (1972) **47**:164
Twickenham (1940) **46**:101
Tychong (1952) **46**:126
Tyndareus **45**:53
Tzelepi (1967) **46**:79
U 36 **46**:118
U 53 **48**:250
U 69 **47**:131
U 72 **46**:118
U 86 **45**:27
U 103 **47**:131
U 107 **46**:119
U 135 **46**:101
U 198 **46**:128
U 752 **45**:51
U 859 **45**:32
UB 14 **48**:259
UB 125 **46**:115
UB Pearl (1973) **48**:241
UB Prudent (1972) **48**:239

UC 65 **47**:177
UC 69 **45**:61
Ulysses **45**:53
Uniceb **45**:36
Unimar (1972) **47**:163
United Drive (1982) **46**:97
United Enterprise (1982)
46:97
United Spirit (1982) **46**:97
United Success (1953)
46:103
United Viscount (1956)
46:75
Uriah M. Rose **45**:22
Urucitrus (1971) **47**:160-1
Uzma (1959) **46**:86
Valsesia (1922) **45**:31-3
Valsugana (1921) **45**:32
Valtellina (1922) **45**:32
Varuna **48**:260
Veejumbo (1959) **48**:202
Vera (1898) **48**:211-2
Veronica (1882) **47**:173,177
Verrazano **45**:36
Vesuv (1881) **48**:210
Victoria (1878) **48**:207
Victoria (1886) **48**:207-8
Victoria (1896) **48**:211
Victoria (1907) **48**:214
Villarperosa (1921) **45**:31-2
Vinashin Pride (1983) **46**:98
Virginia **46**:98
Vista I (1975) **48**:244
Volente (1931) **46**:127
Von der Tann **45**:63
Waimarino (1930) **48**:235
Wameru **45**:29
Wangeroog (1963) **45**:41
War Roach **45**:36
Warwickshire **45**:19
Wen Shui **46**:91
Weng **46**:96
Werkendam **46**:115
West Humhaw **45**:46
West Irmo **45**:46
West Islands (1986) **46**:97
West Kebar **45**:46
West Point (1866) **45**:17
Western Wave (1866)
47:171-2
Weybridge (1958)
46:101;**48**:197
Wild Flamingo (1973) **47**:155
Willapa (USS) (1943) **45**:48
Wimbledon **46**:101
Windsor (1952) **46**:102-3
Windsor Ruby (1981) **46**:98
Windsor Star (1983) **46**:98
Wisbech (1916) **48**:252
Wokingham (1953) **46**:103
Worthing **48**:214
Xin Hai Teng **46**:98
Xin He Er Hao (1973) **46**:97
Yamanashi Maru (1963)
46:68
Yamashiro Maru **46**:68
Yannis (1952) **46**:105
Yewdale (1929) **48**:259
Yi Yang I (1988) **46**:98
Yoma (1958) **48**:202
Yorkshire (3) **45**:19
Yu Xin (1958) **46**:85,94
Yuan Jiang (1981) **46**:97
Yue Yang **46**:98
Zarembo **45**:46
Zealandia **48**:224
Zeila (1963) **46**:124,127
Zheng Yang 2 (1978) **46**:97
Zheng Yang 3 (1981) **46**:97
Zungon (1943) **47**:134
101 (1888) (barge) **45**:60